Matthew Porter tackles v
ficult, often embarrassing
ness and honesty. Drawing
churches to whom St Paul
as a Christian leader and fo
lustrates how giving is not a ~~~~ to be grudgingly fulfilled
but an art to be practised with joy.

David Walker, Bishop of Manchester, UK

This is a thoughtful and insightful book that explores our
calling to be generous givers as part of the way we live out
our faith. It is grounded in biblical study, with helpful personal stories of the challenges and joys of generous giving.
It shows how giving is intrinsic to sharing God's love in our
communities, and how giving transforms the communities we serve, and indeed ourselves, as we discover and re-
discover God's incredible generosity to us.

Jonathan de Bernhardt Wood, National Advisor on Giving
and Income Generation at the Church of England, UK

At Stewardship I am privileged to witness the giving of over
30,000 generous Christians. This book truly captures the
tension they all face between reflecting God's abundant provision and our common worldly sense of lack in these challenging times. It points us beautifully to the right and fitting
solution to this paradox: embracing generosity as a core discipleship habit – such a good gospel message for these days!

Stewart McCulloch, former CEO of Stewardship, now CEO
of Christians Against Poverty

The Art of Giving is a fantastic book to help every disciple of Jesus grow in living a life of generosity with finances and resources. It is easy to read, nuanced and based in the reality of daily life. I am excited to find a book which covers every aspect of giving in an accessible and engaging way. Peppered with inspiring stories from history and the present day which bring the Scriptures alive – this book had me hooked. But perhaps the greatest endorsement I can give is that I know that Matthew, together with his wife Sam, practises what he preaches. I think the reader will be particularly helped by hearing Matthew's journey of growing in the art of giving. I will be recommending that everyone in my church reads this book.

Vicky Earll, Vicar of The Ascension and St Thomas',
Derringham Bank, Hull, UK

This book is a gift to the church because it is both prophetic and practical. Bishop Matthew offers a clear, winsome and joyful call to locate our discipleship around money in the self-giving mercy of Christ and teaches what this might look like in practice.

Brogan Humne, author, Planting Curate at
St Thomas' Newcastle, UK, and Overseer of
New Wine's Discipleship Year intern scheme

The Art of Giving

Becoming a more generous person

Matthew Porter

Authentic

First published 2024 by Authentic Media Limited,
PO Box 6326, Bletchley, Milton Keynes, MK1 9GG.
authenticmedia.co.uk

British Library Cataloguing in Publication Data
A catalogue record for this book is available from the British Library.
ISBN: 978-1-78893-290-5
978-1-78893-291-2 (e-book)

Cover design by Henry Milne
Printed and bound by CPI Group (UK) Ltd, Croydon, CR0 4YY

Contents

Preface

This book is written to help followers of Jesus become more generous through the practice of giving.

It is called *The Art of Giving* because discipleship – the daily practice of following Jesus – is more an art than a science. It's not a technical process, based on logic or analytical deduction. It's not about rigidly adhering to laws or rules about behaviour or piety. It's more like learning a musical instrument, or discovering how to paint, both of which require patient practice. You have to give yourself to it: particularly your energy and emotions, as well as your time and talents. This is the stretching and adventurous life of discipleship into which followers of Jesus are invited, empowered by the Holy Spirit. It's thoroughly relational – loving God and loving people – and beautifully creative, cultivating habits of the heart which result in a lifestyle that brings lasting transformation to us and to the world. Eugene H. Peterson, author of *The Message* version of the Bible, summarised such a life as 'learning the unforced rhythms of grace'.[1]

This book, in *The Art of* series, is about a particular rhythmic feature of discipleship – *The Art of Giving*. In a few pages the habit is explained and explored, with readers encouraged to practise this art in order to mature and impact the world. I think you will enjoy it. But most of all I hope this habit helps you become a more fruitful and fulfilled missional disciple of Jesus.

The Art of Giving is the first in a series of books about discipleship habits.

Matthew Porter
Bishop of Bolton

Introduction

My friend Nick[1] has built a pond. It's a big pond. In fact it looks more like a small lake to me. He lives on a large plot of land so despite the pond's size it doesn't over-dominate and is not out of keeping. He took advice before starting, wanting to know not only where it would best fit in the landscape and what to do to prepare the ground and maintain it, but also needing to be sure it would benefit the ecosystem of the area. He was excited to tell me all about it before he started. As we chatted I asked some questions, including if he planned to have fish. He told me he did, but that he wasn't going to get any. I was confused, so he explained. He said that in time, the fish would just arrive. If a body of water appeared, fish would appear. I thought he was joking, but he was deadly serious. 'They'll just come,' he said, 'normally by eggs in bird or duck droppings. It may take some time, but they'll come. I don't have to do anything, just create the pond.' I was gobsmacked. And now, a few years later, the first signs are already there. From an organism-free start the water is swimming with small aquatic creatures and he's now waiting for the fish. He knows that if he makes a lake, nature will give him fish. It's incredible, but true.

Give!

The story of Nick's lake illustrates something simple but profound: the world thrives on giving. Give a landscape water, and nature gives you fish; fish that reproduce into more fish. Give the earth a seed, and up comes a plant; a plant that produces lots more. Whether it's seed dispersal through birds and fish, water filtration by micro-organisms or tree roots, reproduction through pollination by bees and flies, soil renewal through dung beetles, or pest control by the feeding of parasitic wasps or fungi, scientists have shown us that nature gives. It just does. Giving is how the world grows and prospers. The very fabric of creation works like this, for giving is at the heart of the world in which we live.[2]

Humanity, being part of creation, similarly thrives on giving. In fact we're made to give: to give of our time, energy and resources, investing in our families and communities, our land and businesses. Down the ages many have instinctively understood this – that living a life of giving is the best way to live.[3] Not surprisingly it's central to the beliefs and ethics of many religions, as we're urged to give and contribute to the world and to society, normally with kindness and care honoured, and selfishness discouraged.[4]

If giving really *is* how we thrive, then we'd expect to see it encouraged in all human relationships, especially in marriage, which in most cultures has, alongside singleness, been a basic building block of society.[5] Unsurprisingly, this is exactly what we observe, as our ancestors linked giving to the exchange of wedding rings. Wedding rings are only small, but they say something big – something loud and proud. First and foremost they declare, 'I'm married!' but they also proclaim something deeper about the nature of marriage that's easily missed. Wedding rings shout, 'This marriage is based not on taking, but on giving.' If you don't believe me, google the words of the marriage service. While giving is hinted at in the promises declared in secular venues, it's explicit and central in the ancient vows of the Christian wedding service, particularly as the couple give each other a ring. Here's what they say:

> I give you this ring as a sign of our marriage.
> With my body I honour you,
> all that I am I give to you,
> all that I have I share with you,
> within the love of God,
> Father, Son and Holy Spirit.[6]

As a church leader I've led hundreds of husbands and wives through these words, and every time I do my heart stirs with the profound promises made as together they commit to a union based not on taking, but on giving. Why? Because it's by giving that we live well together, and it's through giving that we change the world.

The importance of giving is a central theme in the Christian Scriptures, with the giving in Christian marriage patterned on the greater giving of Jesus Christ, who sacrificially gave up his life for his bride, the church, whom he loves with a passion.[7] Christ is the image of the giving God[8] who made a universe of plenty.[9] Such is his generosity he's created a bounteous world, overflowing with resources and provision to tend and share and give.[10] Human beings like us are then invited by the Maker to live creatively and generatively in this world – to 'be fruitful and increase' and 'fill the earth'.[11] This is a world that God says is 'very good'.[12] It's a place captured so poignantly and simply in Louis Armstrong's graceful song 'What a Wonderful World'. Welcome to the world of provision, in which we're invited to live a life of giving.

Withhold!

And yet in every society, at all times, there have also been forces at work urging us to view the world differently and *not* to give. They tell us to withhold, because we live in a world of scarcity.[13] In our work, things get hard and difficult. Crops fail, businesses crash and finances get squeezed, so we should hold tight to protect what we have. We switch on the news and most stories are negative – about some problem or issue or scandal. We're presented with a world full of strife and struggle with competing demands that can't be met; we worry that those who give get exploited, and we don't see or believe the resources required are readily available.[14] In our relationships we get cross, we fall out and we break up, and we're then scared to live a life of giving for we fear getting hurt again. We hear a whisper warning us to take care about the vulnerability of love and we become cynical in order to protect our hearts. These are the sights and sounds of the culture of scarcity, informing us that we live in a world where there isn't enough: not enough money; not enough energy; not enough time; not enough anything. And I'm not enough: not smart enough; not pretty enough; not wealthy enough; not good enough. I lack.

Clinical social worker and shame-researcher Brené Brown recognises our not-enough culture and relates the idea of scarcity to shame. 'Shame,' says Brown, 'is the *never good enough* emotion. It can stalk us over time or wash over us in a second – either way, its power to make us feel we're not worthy of connection, belonging, or even love is unmatched in the realm of emotion.'[15] Brown sees shame as the dominant emotion in contemporary Western society, reflecting the culture of scarcity in which we live. For Brown we live in 'a culture of "never enough"'.[16] Lynne Twist sums this up so well when she writes:

> Before we even sit up in bed, before our feet touch the floor, we're already inadequate, already behind, already

losing, already lacking something. And by the time we go
to bed at night, our minds are racing with a litany of what
we didn't get done, that day. We go to sleep burdened by
those thoughts and wake up to that reverie of lack . . . This
internal condition of scarcity, this mind-set of scarcity, lives
at the heart of our jealousies, our greed, our prejudice, our
arguments with life.[17]

As I write this book in the early years of the third decade of
the twenty-first century, the world is still emerging from
the devastating social and economic effects of a two-year
Covid pandemic. To make matters worse, a cost of living
crisis has arisen. Fuel bills have doubled, inflation is at its
highest for years, the economy of the United Kingdom
where I live is struggling, and people fear for their pay and
their jobs. Television news anchors and newspaper jour-
nalists are telling us to tighten our belts, for even harsher
financial times may be ahead.

Dilemma

So which is the correct worldview? Is the world of provision
a fairy story world for children and dreamers, and the world
of scarcity the real world for the shrewd and the sensible?
The answer to these questions is of fundamental importance, as it affects the way we think and live, and especially
the way we give.

This book answers that dilemma by accepting that both worldviews are true and that we must live in the tension of both. If it helps, see the two mindsets as rather like the North and South Poles on the globe, and we're invited to inhabit the space between.[18] This means that on the one hand when we approach a situation, the resources we need may seem lacking, while on the other hand we trust that we have before us everything we need. This space is the prayerful place of trust into which Jesus invites us. It is the kingdom of God. It is the wonderful and playful context of faith, hope and love. For some this is a deeply uncomfortable and risky world of naïve absurdity; for others it's the exciting unknown world of adventurous discipleship. We must acknowledge this tension and be honest about it. And in that pressured place the Spirit of Jesus calls us to start giving.

Key

We give because giving is the key that unlocks the world of provision. It opens the door to divine resources of heaven than can impact earth. Giving releases God's rich realm of abundance to increasingly flow into our flawed and fallen world of lack. This understanding was behind the comment made to me by Bishop Louis Muvunyi, Bishop of Kigali in Rwanda – one of the world's poorest nations – when he said, 'God is showing us that we are rich. That we have all we need.'[19] It's through giving that we access so much of the life of God's kingdom. While this may at first seem counter-intuitive, it's true. But you only discover this by doing it. By giving. St Francis of Assisi realised this, which is why he famously said that 'it's through giving that we receive'.[20]

We don't wait to receive before we give. That's because God has already given us everything we need. The initiative has already been taken by God: in giving us a bounteous world, in giving us Jesus Christ, and in giving us his Holy Spirit, God is supremely generous, being full of grace!

Jesus

Jesus Christ reveals this grace like no other, and is central and paramount to faith, being the all-sufficient, sinless Saviour. His sacrificial death and glorious resurrection have saved us from selfishness and sin, dying the death we deserved. This makes Christ's crucifixion the ultimate act of giving! If we fail to appreciate this, or miss this, we will not understand Christian giving and find it difficult to practise. Indeed without the cross this book would not, and could not, be written.

The church constantly celebrates this self-giving love of Christ in a variety of ways, especially by regularly sharing bread and wine, recalling Jesus' giving of his body and blood for us. Christ's resurrection shows not only that Jesus is alive but also that death could not hold such perfect generosity. As Tim Keller says, the resurrection means we now not only 'have a hope *from* the future but *for* the future'.[21] As we turn to Jesus in repentance and find new identity through his death and resurrection, reorienting our lives around him, so Christ makes us more-than-enough and gives us more-than-enough. Jesus calls us to follow him into a new life of giving, with a new way of thinking and a new set of values.

Value

The new value that summarises the life of giving to which we're called is *generosity*.[22] This is the virtue that Jesus embodied, showing us the gracious giving nature of God,[23] and it's the value that we're asked to bring into every situation, however big or small the need. In many ways *generosity* summarises the whole teaching of Scripture on giving. We're invited to live generously in all aspects of life, as we follow Jesus. When we embrace generosity our response in every context should be: 'how can I help?' and 'how can I serve?' and 'I will give what I can.' As with every virtue, there is a vulnerability to living this way. What if I give and resources run out? Or I give and am exploited? Or I give and become exhausted? These risks are very real and cause many to fear giving, but for those with eyes to see, this is the way of life, for Brené Brown is right when she says that vulnerability really 'is the birthplace of love,

belonging and joy'.[24] That's why we need to learn to practise generosity, living a life of giving in a regular, sustained
and disciplined way.

Discipline

Behind every value there must be a discipline. Michael
Frost has shown this so clearly in his simple but important book *Surprise the World*,[25] saying it's no good artic-
ulating a set of values if they just end up as well-meaning
platitudes on a wall-poster that aren't expressed in reality.
No, values need rooting in every-day life, and the way that
happens is through practising disciplines.

So what discipline is behind generosity? The answer is *financial giving*. Giving away money. This is well expressed
by Archbishop of Canterbury, Justin Welby, who says that
'generosity is seen in the act of giving, not merely in good-
will'.[26] Of course giving money is not the only form of giving, so this book will touch on other aspects of generosity
too. However, the book's main focus is unashamedly on
finances for, as we'll see, giving money is the habit that
opens our hearts to a broader lifestyle of giving. It's as
we give away our money, as an expression of giving our
very selves, that we become God's liberated people who
change the world.

We will see in this book that financial giving is best expressed in five ways – through giving: (1) cheerfully, (2) regularly, (3) occasionally, (4) collectively and (5) expectantly. These five things are thoroughly biblical and have been central to the financial giving of women and men down the ages. They're at the heart of *The Art of Giving* and so provide the five chapters that frame this book.

For some it might help to see these five things like ingredients in a stew. The order may not be particularly important, but we need them all if we're to get the full flavour. That means you can dip into the chapters in any order, and you should still find the book helpful.

Before we begin our first chapter about cheerful giving, there's one further matter to be mentioned by way of introduction, which is about the people from whom we learn. When it comes to financial giving, who is our teacher? This book defaults to Jesus and the Scriptures, which he viewed as authoritative. As a book written by a church leader, you might not find that surprising! But the next statement might, so listen carefully. When Jesus taught about financial giving he told his followers to *watch how people in poverty give, and learn from them*. I didn't always see this, but I do now, and it's a key theme across this book.

Learning

We learn about giving money not by observing the rich give, but by watching the poor.[27] This is profoundly counter-cultural because in most societies it's the giving of rich people that's celebrated, not the meagre offerings of people in poverty. For most of us, not only do we want to avoid *being* poor; we also think there's nothing to learn *from* the poor. Perhaps that explains why in Western culture the giving of rich people has a long and respectable name – called *philanthropy* – while there's no corresponding term for the giving of poor people.[28] It's as if poor people's giving doesn't exist, or it's not important. Jesus begs to differ!

As you'll discover as you read on, there is much to learn about many areas of life from observing poor people, especially about the art of giving.[29] It's the plain reading of what Jesus says in Luke 21:1–4 which, like many Bible teachers and scholars in church history, I see as the prime and controlling text on personal giving in the New Testament.[30] As such it will feature in every chapter of this book. Here's the story.

Sitting down next to the temple treasury in Jerusalem one day with his followers, Jesus watches rich people put their money into the large wooden chests, followed by a poor widow who gives two low-value small copper coins. Jesus then says something astounding: 'This poor widow has put in more than all the others.' In case they weren't sure if he was serious, he prefaces his statement with the words, 'Truly I tell you,' which was Jesus' ways of saying, *Listen up, this is really important and totally true! –* and he then goes on to explain why. The reason, says Jesus, is that 'all these people gave their gifts out of their wealth; but she out of her poverty put in all she had to live on'.

There's lots that can be taken from this story – not just about giving, but also about wealth and poverty.[31] In recent years some have suggested that 'the widow is a victim of oppression, not an example to follow,'[32] with Jesus not commending the widow's actions but instead criticising the Temple and the teachers of the Jewish Law who are encouraging her to give what little she has. There is some wisdom in this, for the context of this story shows that Jesus is standing in the prophetic tradition and exposing the false piety of religious leaders who themselves should be generous.[33] However, I don't accept that Jesus doesn't want her to give, for three reasons. First, Jesus never does this anywhere else. Nowhere in the gospels does Jesus tell people not to give – not even poor people.[34] To do so here would therefore be surprising. Second, as we'll see in this book, giving when resources seem scarce is commended in many places across the breadth of Scripture, so again it would be unusual for Jesus to go against this. In the light of this, and thirdly, if Jesus *is* suggesting her giving is unnecessary, misguided and wrong, we would expect him to say so. But he doesn't.

So what is the meaning of this story? The answer is found in understanding that widows were generally recognised as among the poorest people in society, and yet it's a poor widow who Jesus tells his disciples to notice, pointing out that she gave more than all the others.[35] This means the message is more nuanced than *just be more generous!* Instead, Jesus is saying that *disciples learn generosity by observing the giving of people in poverty.*

Today
Today's cost of living crisis makes many of us feel like we're people in poverty, rather like this widow of Jerusalem. The reality for most of us, however, is that we're not. If you live in the West and are reading this book, you are well-off. Compared with most people alive today, and those who've shared this planet with us in the past, the majority of us are rich. There are of course people in every cultural context who struggle financially and who might be deemed 'poor' according to certain indices. More economic poor people have been created by the present rise in living costs, and this book suggests that we can learn from their giving, as we can learn from the generosity of the widow of Jerusalem, because she was living in a *permanent* cost of living crisis! Indeed, that's the daily experience of people in

poverty, which is another reason why we master the discipline of giving, especially in difficult economic days, not by emulating rich givers but *poor* givers. They fully understand what it feels like to lack resources, yet they still give.

So this book called *The Art of Giving* is unashamedly about financial giving. It encourages readers to become givers and to learn from the generosity of poor givers, so we might become Christ's generous, missional disciples and discover the joy of giving again and again. As you read and put what it says into practice, be prepared to go on a generosity journey that'll be enriching and demanding. Anything of value is like that, and giving is of immense worth.

Like all the books in this series, this book is fairly short and won't take long to read. If you have questions about it, or you'd like to share stories and testimonies, do contact me. I'd be pleased to hear from you. You can email me at bishopmatthew@manchester.anglican.org.

Enjoy *The Art of Giving!*

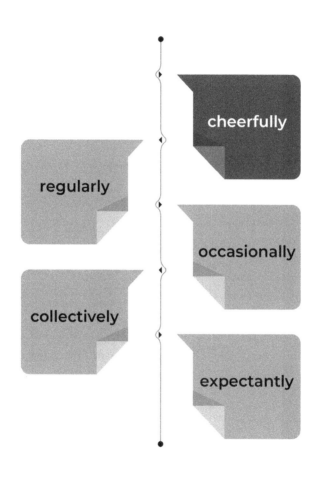

Chapter 1

cheerfully

- *'God loves a cheerful giver' (2 Corinthians 9:7).*

- *'The joy of the LORD is your strength' (Nehemiah 8:10).*

- *'And what are these joys that the Lord gives us? Only one drop of water from the great, overflowing river that he has prepared for us' (Teresa of Avila).*[1]

- *'When we give cheerfully and accept gratefully, everyone is blessed' (Maya Angelou).*[2]

Spider Man. Back to the Future. You Only Live Twice. Dead Man Walking. True Lies. Eyes Wide Shut. They're all titles of successful films. Film titles are big business. The wrong title on the wrong film can create a flop, but a good title, while not guaranteeing a great film, catches our attention and makes us want to know more. That's why the movie industry will pay for an appealing title, and sometimes that title – like all those above – is an oxymoron. An oxymoron is an apparent contradiction. Logically it doesn't make sense, but we're intrigued and drawn in by the clever use of conflicting words.

Embedded within the New Testament's longest and clearest teaching on financial giving (in 2 Corinthians 8 and 9) is a five-word phrase: 'God loves a cheerful giver.'[3] It's a warm encouragement to give with joy. With gladness. With a smile on our faces and love in our hearts. But in many people's minds, *giving cheerfully* is an oxymoron. It seems irrational that giving away our hard-earned money could ever be cheerful, happy or jolly! Surely giving is *losing*. It's taking away – subtracting, extracting and detracting. How can we do that cheerfully? Others see giving as rather like paying taxes. They know it's necessary and even good for society but they do it rather reluctantly, through gritted teeth. If honest they'd rather not do it at all, or certainly would like to contribute less, for that way they'd have more. However you look at it, many don't view giving positively. It just feels like yet another bill to pay.

So why should we give cheerfully and how can we do that with integrity? That's what this first chapter is all about, for cheerfulness is meant to be at the centre of good giving.

Dancing

In the last ten years I've had the privilege of visiting two of the most beautiful countries in the world – Burundi and Rwanda. As well as sharing a border in East Africa, they both enjoy a climate that's warm in the day and cool at night, with some rain too, so the land is fertile and productive. They've had their share of troubles and tensions, culminating in the horrific genocide in 1994. There's much being done to ensure that never happens again, and when I visited I met wonderful people who are rebuilding their nations with kind hearts. Both countries, especially Burundi, are among the poorest on the planet, and yet I've seen in the churches there a generosity in poverty that has been profoundly moving and deeply challenging. In most communities the churches play an important role, offering compassionate social action programmes, caring for those in need and offering practical training in a breadth of issues, from health and family life, to business and lifestyle skills. Lots of churches do this despite having very little, and it's wonderful to see. Another thing I discovered is the unexpected way the financial offering is taken in some of the churches – by dancing. Yes, dancing! In the context of their vibrant worship, where all ages love to sing and clap and praise God using rhythm and harmony, in many churches when it's time to give, people dance their way to the front and place their financial gifts on the offering plate with huge smiles, as everyone claps and celebrates God's goodness and provision. The first time I saw this I was surprised by the contrasting emotions I felt, for while I loved their joyful giving I was also shocked, for I'd never before seen people give in this way. It contrasted so starkly with the dull offering times I'd seen so often in the UK church. Here I observed people celebrating their offerings to God. They were, it seemed, genuinely pleased to give.

Free-will

Cheerful giving is about finding pleasure in generosity. It's not giving just because you *have* to, but because you *want* to.

This was modelled for us like no other by Jesus Christ, in his death on the cross. Yes, he struggled knowing the pain he would have to endure,[4] but in the end he willingly and gladly gave up his life for our salvation, with Hebrews 12:2 saying, 'For the joy that was set before him he endured the cross.' He could have chosen otherwise, but instead he voluntarily walked the path to which God was calling him, seeing the end result and the benefits. The benefits of his giving were, of course, mainly for others, with New Testament scholar F.F. Bruce saying that '"the joy set before him" is not something for himself alone, but something to be shared with those for whom he died as sacrifice and lives as high priest'.[5] So it was with joy that Jesus offered himself.

St Michael le Belfrey, the church which I led in York for thirteen years, is an Anglican church and part of the Diocese of York. The diocese is the parent body that funds the salary of paid clergy in the parishes and supports local churches in a variety of ways, especially those in areas of deprivation. In response, each parish is invited to contribute a freewill offering to fund the work of the diocese. It's not a tax, it's an offering. It's giving. The Belfrey has been pleased to do this, seeking each year to give to the diocese much more than received. Despite it being an offering, I would sometimes hear people in diocesan meetings talking about people *paying* their contribution to the diocese rather than *giving*, and when I did it always grated, for we weren't supposed to be paying, but giving. The two things are very different! Maybe it's revealing, for the language of 'payment' sometimes betrays the heart not just of a dutiful giver but of a reluctant giver.

Why

Maybe you're reading this book because you're a reluctant giver. When you give you feel conflicted and uncomfortable and sometimes even pained to let go of your money. To be totally honest, most givers understand *something* of this. I've been giving for many years but even today I occasionally hear a voice inside my head reminding me what else I could do with that money: the gift I could buy; the holiday we could go on; or the so-called 'security' I could have, knowing the bank account is well in credit. If we're to give cheerfully and live a lifestyle of generosity, we have to drown those voices by attending to a different sound: the joyful sound that reminds us why it's good to give. Here are three key reasons why:

1. **My giving reveals what I love.** Our giving helpfully exposes our passions and priorities.[6] Show me your bank statements and you show me what you really think is important.

2. **My giving transforms me.** While giving should always be motivated by the help it can bring to others[7] it also changes us and is good for us.[8] It benefits both the recipient *and* the giver.[9]

3. **My giving transforms the world.** If we want to see positive change, we must become givers. Giving impacts the future – here on earth and into eternity.[10] Jonathan de Bernhardt Wood, the Church of England's National Advisor on Giving, is very clear on this, saying to me, 'It's the best way to "spend" our money, meaning more to those we give it to than it ever could to us, and achieving more.'[11]

There are more reasons than these, but they're a good start. And they're true. My giving shows what I think is important, for I can't give to everything. My giving also changes me for good, in all sorts of positive ways. And my giving *really does* transform people and the world. It allows them to do what they otherwise would not be able to do.

Jesus encourages his followers to give in all sorts of ways. As we'll see in this book, he tells stories. He speaks words of truth. He demonstrates generosity in the way he lives. He also gives five very clear *don'ts*, which when placed together are stark and helpful. Here they are:

1. **Don't announce your giving to be honoured by others** (Matthew 6:2–3).
   Instead, give generously without making a fuss.

2. **Don't store up treasures on earth** (Matthew 6:19–21).

   Instead 'store up for yourselves treasures in heaven'. Give to things that will last for eternity. Think long term. The benefit for everyone, including you, will be greater.

3. **Don't worry about money or your basic needs** (Matthew 6:25–33).

   Instead 'seek first his kingdom and his righteousness, and all these things will be given to you as well'. He will take care of the generous.

4. **Don't take money or much provision when on mission** (Luke 9:3; 10:4).

   Instead, be vulnerable and trust God to provide. This will stretch your faith in wonderful ways.

5. **Don't be foolish and store up riches only for yourself** (Luke 12:16–21).

   Instead, be 'rich towards God' and be on your guard against greed and accumulating 'an abundance of possessions'. Less is more.

For all these reasons and more, we need to learn to give, and to do so confidently, heartily and gladly, with a big smile on our faces!

Philippi

A church that particularly models cheerfulness in the Bible is the church of Philippi. Founded about AD 50 by the apostle Paul following the clear guidance of the Holy Spirit, it was the first European church.[12] When in prison some twelve years later[13] Paul wrote a letter to this church – which we call *Philippians* – and it's part of the New Testament. Paul's passion for this church is self-evident from the start of his letter, for he writes and says, 'in all my prayers for all of you I always pray with joy'[14] and later he calls them 'my joy and crown'.[15] On a number of occasions he articulates his desire to 'rejoice'[16] and he invites them to 'rejoice with me'.[17] In the final chapter Paul writes vulnerably about his life in prison, saying, 'I have learned to be content whatever the circumstances . . . whether living in plenty or want.'[18] And then he thanks them for their past and present financial support of him, which he describes as 'a fragrant offering, an acceptable sacrifice, pleasing to God'.[19] As a result Paul tells them that 'my God will meet all your needs according to the riches of his glory in Christ Jesus'.[20] Joy and provision have overflowed between Paul and this church, so much so that even in the midst of scarcity in prison, Paul can say he has 'more than enough'.[21] Their cheerful giving has released the kingdom of abundance to him, bringing contentment and joy. This is what cheerful giving does. Joy begets joy.

York

In 2021 I announced to the church family at St Michael le Belfrey that we'd been given an extraordinary gift of one million pounds to set up a Love York Post-Pandemic Fund.

People were excited about how we could help people in our city recover well from the difficult pandemic period, and there was much rejoicing. But the thing I remember most about announcing the gift was a conversation I had immediately afterwards. It was with someone, let's call him Brian, who asked if he could contribute to the fund. I know Brian quite well. He and his family live on a low income with little disposable income. Brian came bounding up to me and said, 'This is *so* good! I'm really thrilled we have this gift. Please can I contribute and add to the fund?' Knowing that his gift might well be just a few pounds, I said with all sincerity, 'Brian, that would be great. Thank you so much. We'd be honoured.' I don't know how much Brian gave, but probably in human terms his gift would have been miniscule compared with the main donation, but I know it was given from a cheerful, generous heart, and I believe to this day that his additional gift was as significant in God's kingdom as the million-pound gift, for as well as being given out of poverty, it was given cheerfully.

Widow

According to Jesus, giving out of poverty is how the widow of Jerusalem gives when she comes to the temple to worship.[22] We're not told much information about her, but given that she comes to worship and gives all she has, we should assume she's a devout Jew. She has probably heard the psalms read on many occasions and would know Psalm 100, which says, 'Worship the LORD with glad-ness; come before him with joyful songs.'[23] I'd like to think this is her attitude when she comes to the great temple in Jerusalem to worship. And then she approaches the temple treasury to offer her financial gifts, for worship and giving always go together. The two are always inextrica-bly linked in the Bible,[24] which Jewish people understood, so it's likely that both her praises *and* her financial gifts are all given 'with gladness'. Even though she has little – just two small copper coins – she still gives. I like to think she's pleased to give, giving cheerfully as part of her wor-ship and giving in response to the generosity of God. If so, she gives out of loving-obedience, which explains why she gives everything she has.

This kind of cheerful giving in poverty became a mark of the earliest Christian believers after Pentecost. In Acts Luke tells us that people in the Jerusalem church 'had everything in common', seeing their possessions as being available to help their needy brothers and sisters.[25] That's why some shared resources, voluntarily selling property and land. The intention was certainly to help alleviate pov-erty but it's likely that many gave sacrificially and some in-tentionally made themselves poor. Luke says they did all this cheerfully and gladly, being 'one in heart and mind'.[26] The Macedonian church, as we'll see in chapter four, were poor and yet also gave with 'overwhelming joy'.[27] But the best example, as we've seen, is the church in Philippi. Even though they suffered for their faith,[28] they continued to rejoice and to live generously, giving away the gospel in word and action,[29] and especially through their financial giving.

Power

When we give cheerfully – with joy like the church in Philippi, with loving-obedience like the widow of Jerusalem, and with dancing like the church in Burundi – we're doing something incredibly powerful. We're defying the power of money. It's not in control. In fact we take charge of money, rather than letting money take charge of us. This is very important, as money has the potential to rule us. Jesus knew this, which is why he declared with crystal clarity, 'You cannot serve both God and money.'[30] His weighty statement has led to the creation of a spectrum of views about the nature of money. At one end some have viewed money as evil and to be used with great caution, and at the other it's seen positively and so should be used well. Many today sit somewhere in the middle, considering money to be amoral or neutral; it all depends on what you do with it.[31] Despite the variety of views, all would agree that money is powerful and that human hearts are easily corrupted by it, so we must take care not to let money take hold of us.[32] This book advises that the best way to do that is to live a life of giving. While we must be generous with our time, energy and love, something particularly shifts when we give money, especially when *we* ourselves are in poverty or financially stretched. We're showing it's not in charge. Giving takes the sting out of money, breaking its hold and defying its power.

We see this in the giving of the Antioch church (in Acts 11), which we'll examine in more detail in chapter three. When they discovered a cost of living crisis was coming, instead of holding back their giving, they stepped up and gave generously. Instead of worrying about being poor, they became concerned about the needs of others. With the prospect of poverty looming, they showed great generosity.

This is why it's helpful to observe the giving of people in poverty. We learn so much from them about how to give generously and cheerfully. I saw this first-hand in Burundi in 2014. One hot Sunday morning a group of eight of us joined in the worship of a poor church community in a small rural village. The worship was strong and all ages were present. The local people had heard that visitors were coming and they were delighted to have us, especially all the way from the UK. To our surprise at the end of the service they gave us all a gift – of ice-cold bottles of Coke and Fanta. On such a warm day they were a kind and expensive gift. When they brought them out, with smiles on their faces, my heart was torn. I was thirsty and it was just what I needed, but I also felt deeply uncomfortable about receiving such a gift from people who were much poorer than me. Surely they should have them? We could just go and buy some later, after the service. One of our party, who'd been to Burundi before, noticed my reluctance and leaned over and whispered to me, 'Drink it. You must drink it. We are their guests and they're showing hospitality to us. It's important for them. And it's important for us to receive their hospitality. So drink!' Suitably chastised, I drank, and it was just what I needed. But it took me a while to really grasp how important this was for them to give, and for me to receive. They were genuinely pleased to give to us, even though it stretched them, and afterwards I realised it showed equality and a common bond of inter-dependence. Like the widow of Jerusalem and the Macedonian churches, they gave from their poverty. And like the church of Philippi, they gave cheerfully.

Thankful

Giving cheerfully is not just what Christians in poverty are called to do; it's what we're *all* invited to enjoy doing. This came across to me so clearly a few years ago when I went to visit a couple to ask a financial favour. It's rare for me to ask for money from anyone – for myself or my church – but on this occasion, after consideration and prayer, I went to see a couple in church who'd said to me in the past that if the church needed help with anything, I should ask them. We were in a period of growth in the student ministry at The Belfrey at that time, and along with the leadership team I felt we needed to employ a full-time student worker, but our day-to-day budget could not stretch to do this. So I visited the couple in their home and explained the vision for the role and the need, and that we could only do it with some extra financial support, and I asked if they would consider helping. They listened well and responded with good questions, including clarification on how much was needed. Eventually they said this: 'We don't need further time to think about it. We love what's happening among the students and we can see the role is needed. So we'd be happy to support the post. Just send us a follow-up email confirming all the information you've shared. That's all we need. We'd be pleased to finance this for three years. And we'd love to support it in full, so you don't have to worry about the budget.' I sat there amazed, as deep down I thought they might say no, or maybe at best they'd support half the post. I was *so* thankful, and I'm sure they could tell by my thankful prayers that I prayed before I left! But the thing I remember most about the conversation is what they said at the door, as I was leaving. With a big smile on their faces, they said this: 'Matthew, thank you for coming to see us. We are really pleased to help. Thank you for asking us.'

Self-righteousness

Giving is a privilege. It's an honour to be asked. To join in with God's work in God's world by giving money is a great and noble thing. It's not about the amount, it's about the heart behind it. As we give, we do so in loving-obedience and with a cheerful heart, for as Pete Greig says, 'We are called to dispense joy.'[33]

It's important to recognise that giving thankfully and cheerfully like this, and being pleased to do so, is not the same as giving self-righteously. We don't pat ourselves on the back and say how well we've done. Jesus was very clear about this,[34] for in his culture many liked to show off their piety or good deeds, which still can be the case today. If that's our aim then our motives are wrong. As we've seen in this chapter, we give cheerfully as part of our worship of God, to make a difference in the world, and to help others. There are benefits that come back to us, which we'll explore in more detail in chapter five, but we don't give to get. We give to bless. To help. To transform. That's why we can dance down the aisle and give with exceeding joy.

- give cheerfully because you want to, out of loving-obedience

- give cheerfully, because you see the difference it makes

- cheerful giving is radical; it defies the power that money can hold on us

- cheerful giving is what Christians do, even when times are tough

- cheerful giving liberates us to trust in God

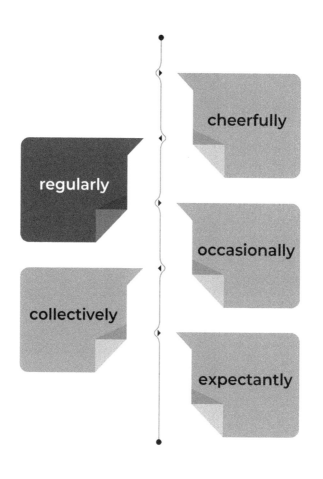

Chapter 2

- *'On the first day of every week, each one of you should set aside a sum of money in keeping with your income' (1 Corinthians 16:2).*

- *'Honour the LORD with your wealth, with the firstfruits' (Proverbs 3:9).*

- *'Christians are not fearless hoarders; we are fearless givers' (Rosario Butterfield).*[1]

- *'Your habits are not the only actions that influence your identity, but by virtue of their frequency they are usually the most important ones' (James Clear).*[2]

When I was a child I loved the story of *The Hare and the Tortoise*, but I didn't believe it. It's one of Aesop's Fables, a collection of fictional tales attributed to a Greek slave who lived in the sixth century BC. In the story the hare and the tortoise decide to race. The hare sets off at a fast pace and is so confident of winning that he stops to take a nap midway through. When he awakens and then reaches the finishing line he finds the slow-moving tortoise has already arrived and he's lost the race. It's a simple story with a memorable message that slow and steady is better than fast and furious. I remember teachers at my junior school talking about it and speaking of the value of consistent discipline over erratic bursts. It all sounded good and I thought it was a nice story; I just didn't think it was true in reality. I was sure that ninety-nine times out of a hundred, the hare would win. Since then I've reflected on *The Hare and the Tortoise* a number of times, and I still agree with my eight-year-old self: the hare should win every time, but only if it keeps going.

Keeping going is highly underrated. As Aristotle said, 'We are what we repeatedly do. Excellence, then, is not an act, but a habit.'[3] So whether you're fast or slow, pressing on and doing something again and again has great benefit, especially when it's a habit or discipline of value. Giving is like that. As Adam Grant says, 'Over time, giving may build willpower like weight lifting builds muscle.'[4] It's of great value, which is why this chapter is all about giving regularly, and how we do that consistently and well.

Planning

Even before it was published in 2013, Susan Caine's book *Quiet* was making a noise. As an introvert in a world that celebrates extroversion, Caine decided she was going to research and then write about the benefits of being thoughtful and reflective. When news about it reached the book-world, a bidding war began among publishers. They sensed a best-seller and they weren't wrong, for Caine's timely and important book revealed not only that some of the greatest influencers in many walks of life have been introverts – such as Mahatma Gandhi, Eleanor Roosevelt, Charles Darwin, Dr Seuss, Rosa Parks, Albert Einstein, Steve Wozniak, Steven Spielberg, and J.K. Rowling – but also that many 'quiet' character traits are powerfully transformative and helpful in lots of fields. These characteristics include studying, planning, inventing, meditating, designing, thinking and cooking. They also include doing things regularly. This means that some personality types will find giving regularly to be straightforward and easy; once they see the benefit they'll get on and do it. And then there are others. They know they should give regularly, and even want to give regularly, but they never get round to it. If that's you, don't skip over this chapter on planning to give as it may be the one you need to read the most, for as Benjamin Franklin rightly said, 'Failing to plan is planning to fail.'[5]

Corinth

From the earliest days of the church, Christ-followers were told to plan their regular giving. In a city where people were paid weekly, Paul wrote to the church in Corinth and said, 'On the first day of the week, each one of you should set aside a sum of money in keeping with your income.'[6] This means that after pay-day we're to give, and we're to do so regularly – week after week, or month after month. This is what the Corinthian church was urged to do, and they're this chapter's key church, who were especially taught to give regularly. They probably didn't do it very well, which explains why Paul guides them. In many ways they're like us – they're people learning to give.

If you have a bank account, giving regularly is relatively straightforward to do in these days of standing orders and digital banking apps; you can set up a regular gift in just a couple of minutes and out it goes from your account at intervals determined by you. Some organisations, such as the Church of England for whom I work, encourage giving at source (i.e. coming directly from your pay), which has some benefits for both the recipient and the giver. However you do it, the main thing is to give, and to do so regularly.

Questions

So let's get practical, and address three very common questions about regular giving: How much? Who to? And, how often?

The best way I can answer these questions is by telling you what Sam and I do. That way you can see how this works out in a particular life and family. We've been married since

1990 and as I'll explain, we were also giving regularly as individuals before then, so we've been doing this for a while now. In our marriage we share financial decisions, so the story will be about 'we' and 'us', but the principles apply just the same to individuals. In telling our giving story, in no way are we suggesting we do this perfectly and we're certainly not suggesting we're model givers. No doubt there are many who are much more generous than we are, and we're still learning and growing in our giving. Nevertheless, what we've discovered is that pursuing generosity is one of the joys of life and, if we could, we'd give away more. That's why one of our goals together in life is to try to give away more each year than the previous one. The most effective way we've discovered to do that is by giving regularly.

How much?

This is usually the first question. How much should I give?

Everything

Sam and I have found that the answer to this question depends on your world-view about life. Why am I alive, and what's important? And, most significantly, is there a God who not only made the world and us, but who gives direction to us about how we live and give? If you're unsure about those questions then the amount you give may be determined by how effectively a charity pulls on your emotional heart-strings, or the algorithm feed of news on your phone, or the little that's left in your bank account before pay day.

As we've seen in our first chapter, followers of Jesus have a Christ-shaped worldview, believing that the God revealed in Christ made the universe, created each one of us, and placed us on planet Earth for a purpose. For all its beauty, we and creation are fallen and broken, which is why he sent Jesus to put things right. As his forgiven and Spirit-filled followers he wants to help us bring transformation to our world of seeming scarcity, and central to that is choosing to give generously with his resources. Giving, and giving in a disciplined way, is basic to the life of discipleship to which we're called.

All this means that *everything* we have belongs to God. He created all that's good, and it's his. He made us, and we are his. This is what the Bible says.[7] Sam and I believe this, which means that all resources, including our money, our home and our lives themselves are his. One hundred per cent. It also means that we're not to see our giving as 'God's' and the rest as 'ours'. No, it's *all* his; it's just he's given responsibility for some of his resources to us for a while. The idea behind this is sometimes known as *stewardship*. We're stewards of God's resources.[8]

So when we come to the question of 'How much?' the short answer is *everything*. As I've occasionally said in a talk on giving, 'When the collection bag comes round, get in!' for we're called to give our very selves to God, which means that we give our all. That's our daily prayer and

consistent song.[9] We're surrendered servants and dedicated disciples, and from that place of submission we
open the Scriptures, and there we see an invitation to live
generously with everything we have – from our time and
energy to our money. For me, though, I learned this initially
not so much from the Bible, but from observing my family.

Noticing

Richard and Christine Porter, my parents, were a
generous-hearted couple. We didn't eat out often as a
family, but when we did they'd always leave a good tip, and
when on holiday I saw that on the day we were checking
out they'd give a little extra to staff who'd served us. When
we went to the market early on Christmas Eve to pick
up final things for the festive season, Dad would pay the
stall-holders, thank them for looking after us during the
past year and then put an extra bank-note in their hand as
a Christmas gift. I noticed these things. Also, at home there
was often an extra place set at evening meal, as my parents opened the home to people who lived on their own or
maybe were visiting from overseas, and guests from a variety of backgrounds would also sometimes stay over in our
house. I later discovered that Jesus had much to say about
generous giving[10] and hospitality,[11] and that he loved to be
welcomed into people's homes to eat and talk and pray.[12]
When Sam and I married and set up home together, we
tried to do the same in our household. We have regularly

invited guests to eat with us, and we enjoy getting to know people over a meal, as well as listening to and supporting those who are struggling, and do this regularly. We've had people stay with us who are in difficulties, including a mother and son escaping domestic violence, a teenage unaccompanied refugee, someone with little income but a call to serve in our church's House of Prayer, and someone going through a difficult relationship breakdown. We especially look out for people each year who'll be on their own on Christmas Day and Easter Day and we love to welcome them into our home and family. We probably could do more, and we know others who do, but our aim is to do what we can, and to use the resources we've been given to help others. I learned that from, and saw that in, my parents. For most people, our family of origin is particularly formative, causing us to see the world in a particular way. Our family is the place where the creating and shaping of many values and practices takes place.

My parents gave by weekly envelope to their church, gave us money to put in the Sunday collection plate at church, and they also supported quite a number of missionaries and missionary societies. I know they were generous in giving money – to church and to others – but they rarely talked about financial giving and I can't recall asking about it. Perhaps it was because they were from a generation where what you did with money was deemed to be private or personal. Looking back now, I wish they'd said more that would have filled in some holes in my understanding. That gap, however, was helpfully met by people at church when I was at university in Nottingham. I watched what they did with their money and I asked them about it. I noticed that some people in our small group would pray when they were in financial need, and they'd give thanks when the Lord provided. They had an expectation that God would look after them, especially as they lived generous lives. As a result, I took the decision at university to start giving money regularly, choosing to give ten per cent of my income away to my local church, and if possible to other things in addition, as and when I could. Regular giving in this way was the foundational discipline I put in place that I hoped would enable me to build a life of generous giving.

Tithing

After I'd started giving regularly like this for a few months, I discovered this was called *tithing*. Even though my income wasn't high as a student, this felt like a big stretch. I initially gave towards the end of each term, trying to ensure I had enough money left over to give, but eventually I realised it was much better to give as soon as I received the money, and then seek to live off the remainder. Not only was that sensible, as I could clearly see what was left, I realised it was also a step of faith, trusting that the remainder would be enough to live on. And it was. It was enough. So that's what Sam and I have done ever since, giving at least a tithe of our income by standing order as soon as we're paid. As I dug deeper into the Bible I discovered that giving *the first* ten per cent like this is encouraged in a number of places; it's called giving the 'first-fruits' as an offering to the Lord, and it goes right back before the giving of the Mosaic law, to Abraham.[13] As God's people did this they trusted that God would look after them in response to their generosity. For Sam and me, this has always been our experience. We have never lacked.

There have, however, been many times when finances have been tight. Very tight. Especially as our family grew to a family of seven, and as we sometimes had others come to live with us and our five children. Occasionally money felt so scarce that I didn't think we would be able to manage. While we prayed daily for the Lord to help, giving us each day our daily bread, on many occasions we had to ask the Lord to provide beyond our means. A few times we had bills on the car that we were unable to pay, and payments on a holiday booked months before that we thought we could fund but we couldn't now afford. This is despite having a budget, seeking to live carefully, not making silly big purchases and, most importantly, aiming to live generously. When we lived in Sheffield from 1996 to the end of 2008 sometimes people would come to the door in need, and we would empty our cupboards of some of the food we'd bought for ourselves, having to trust that we would have enough for that week or month, and we always did. While there was always the option to reduce our regular financial giving, or ask family or friends for monetary help,[14] we have never felt comfortable doing either. Instead we've prayed. Often we've asked our children to pray with us when we needed money, so that when the answer came, they would know that they'd played a part in seeing the answer come about. As a result we've had tax rebates come out of the blue. A few times people have sent us cheques in the post and a couple of times money has come in an envelope through the letter box. Once someone bought us a car. On a number of occasions people have paid for holidays for us.[15] We have always had more than enough, and it feels like the Lord has honoured our desire to be generous.

Starting

If you want to be generous, start giving regularly. Just start. That's what we've learned. Set up a standing order and give. And don't think pounds, think *per cent*. You might only be able to give a few per cent at first, but if that's the case begin with that. That's what we did at St Chad's Church in Sheffield when I became vicar in 2000. When I arrived the church gave away less than one per cent of its income from its annual budget. I understood the difficulties and that after paying bills we had little left over, but in the end what we gave just didn't seem generous. As we prayed and asked for the guidance of the Spirit, I told the Church Council that we needed to grow – in numbers, in maturity, in income *and* in our giving – and that we needed to be intentionally generous in our financial planning. Yes, we needed to ask the church family to give generously to church but also, *we* needed to model that collectively by what we gave away as a church. In essence, we needed to plan our giving and trust that we could survive, and hopefully thrive, on the remainder.

So when we set our church budget the following year I proposed that we should give five per cent of our income away, and increase it each year by one per cent until we got to ten per cent and then review things. Jumping to five per cent was a big stretch, but we agreed, and at the end of that year we broke even. Amazing! So the following year we gave six per cent, as agreed, and we broke even again. We did the same the next year, giving seven per cent. Interestingly, we never did give eight, or even nine per cent, because the year after giving seven per cent we jumped again – all the way to ten per cent! Why? Because we noticed that every year we gave more, we received more, and it felt like the Lord was honouring our giving. This didn't mean the decisions were easy, for our income was rising, which meant the amount we were giving away was increasing too, so the risks were becoming greater. Jumping from seven to ten per cent felt like a huge prophetic step of faith, similar to going from one per cent to five had been, and we had to trust that the Lord would provide. And he did. We could now support more evangelistic work and begin to help people working in areas of poverty like never before, and it was great! Interestingly, the proposal to jump from seven per cent to ten didn't come from me. It came from someone on the Church Council who had observed how God had honoured our giving, and so they challenged us to press on and tithe as a church. We took this faith-step and it was worth it. I sometimes tell this story to individuals or families who want to give more, encouraging them to do something similar.[16] Give something, and then each year reassess and try to increase, say, by one per cent each year, aiming to reach at least a tithe over time. Normally we can. And the benefits are great.

Miranda is a church member known to me who became a follower of Jesus as a young mother. Her husband wasn't sure about faith, and after many years of her faithful prayer and witness he's recently decided for himself that he wants to become a believer. In the intervening years, Miranda understood that disciples are called to be generous givers and so she wanted to give regularly by giving ten per cent of her income. Her husband disagreed. They shared financial decisions and money was tight, and he couldn't understand why this was important. So in the end, she decided to begin by giving something – and that was to give ten per cent of the government child benefit, giving £5 a week to church. Even though she would have loved to give more, this still felt important and it was indeed a huge step of faith for her. She later told me, 'I think it was the regular commitment and the heart behind it, more than the actual figure, that the Lord was interested in.' Miranda believes that God honoured the fact that she started giving in this way and that she did so regularly. While they've never been well off, Miranda tells me they've never gone without and always had more than enough.

So how much we give is up to us. The important thing is to give something. And aim for ten per cent, which is a good starting point for giving, recognising that the remainder also still belongs to the Lord.

Who To?

A second giving question is 'Who should I give to?'

As Sam and I have considered this question over the years, we've together come to two somewhat contradictory conclusions. On the one hand it doesn't matter too much what or to whom you give to, as long as they're a worthy cause. The most important thing is to give, especially if you're a disciple of Jesus, because giving is what disciples do.

It's basic to our faith. So give. And give joyfully, in such a way that it brings transformation. The bi-product of giving cheerfully and regularly is that the habit will form us into generous people for, as James Clear – an expert on habits and decision-making – advocates, our habits build values that shape our identity.[17] On the other hand, the Scriptures guide us to a primary channel for our giving, which followers of Jesus should take seriously – and that's through the local church. It's the local church where the tithe belongs. According to Carl Bates, 'God has always had a "place" for holy money to be put. In the Old Testament that place was the Tabernacle and the Temple. In the New Testament that place was and is the church.'[18] R.T. Kendall concurs, saying, 'The tithe is to be *entrusted* to the Church that the Church may make the proper decision as to its use.'[19] This 'not only supports the ministry of that church but provides funds for that particular church to turn to send the Gospel around the world'.[20] Sam and I agree, which is why we've always done this. We give at least a tithe of our gross income away to the local church. We also give to other things but the foundation of our giving – at least ten per cent – is to the local church. We do this because we believe the local church is the most significant body for transformation on the planet. This is not to denigrate other arenas, for politics, education, business and the charitable sector are examples of other key areas of influence. But in the end, there's nothing like the local church, in its diversity, creativity and missional endeavour. That's why we pray that every local community in our region will benefit from a strong local church. It's why I'm now a bishop, as I want to play my part in encouraging and strengthening local parishes and churches in the Manchester area. God believes in and has instituted the local church, and invites us to co-labour with him in giving generously there. If every Christ-follower did this, the majority of the financial issues in most churches would disappear, but most importantly the church could be so much more effective in its mission, both locally and beyond.

I write this very aware that I am a church leader who's paid by the church, which means I have an interest that I must declare! But Sam and I gave to our local church before I was a church leader, and when I retire we aim to do the same, so we don't tithe just to help ourselves; rather, we tithe as an act of loving-obedience. We give at least ten per cent to our church, doing what Malachi 3 says: 'Bring the whole tithe into the storehouse, that there may be food in my house.' Anything less, Malachi says, is 'robbing God', which are strong words, telling us in no uncertain terms that the tithe belongs in the place of worship.[21] As we give, we trust that the local church will use the money wisely and well. After all, as my friend Brogan Hume once said to me, 'If you don't trust your local church with ten per cent of your money, why do you trust them with your discipleship?'!

The Church of England, through its General Synod, presently recommends that people split their tithe, giving five per cent to the local church, and five per cent to charities. While this approach is commendable, we don't do that. We have always believed that the tithe belongs in the local church and so our baseline for church giving is always at least ten per cent, and then giving to good causes is in addition. Don't forget that if your local church is missional then a good chunk of your church giving will support good causes, which probably include things local, regional, national and international, such as food banks and overseas mission partners.

Revealing

As disciples, we're called together and individually to be givers, not takers. To help us understand this, the gospel accounts intentionally present us with the character of Judas, whose attitude to money makes uncomfortable reading, for he developed the art of taking rather than giving. He was put in charge of Jesus' money bag, but as a thief he helped himself to what was put in it.[22] Money corroded his heart, polluted his mind and tainted his actions.[23] Mark's gospel tells us it was an extreme act of generosity by a woman called Mary, who poured an extraordinary amount of very expensive perfume on Jesus, that triggered Judas' betrayal of Jesus. Judas saw it as a ludicrous 'waste' while Jesus received Mary's perfume as 'beautiful' and an act of extravagant adoration.[24] When money becomes our idol, generous giving becomes insufferable. As our god, money produces death not life. This was Judas' story, and it's what he's remembered for: the death of Jesus, followed by his own death by suicide.[25] The love of money got a grip on his life, stained his heart and revealed what he loved. Aware of Judas' story, disciples of Jesus are instead called to react differently, so that when money reveals selfishness and greed we acknowledge this to ourselves and to God. We repent and invite the Spirit of Jesus to bring transformation. This can be painful, requiring honest reflection in prayer, which can be aided by confession and reflection through journalling,[26] as we are attentive to our hearts.

When I was first a vicar there was a financial need in our church, and so I asked the Lord in prayer for a specific sum of money to help. A couple of weeks later someone I know, unaware of my prayer and unconnected to the church, wrote to me enclosing a cheque, saying they'd come into some money and felt prompted to send some of it to me. I was delighted, for the cheque inside was for the exact amount I had prayed for! However, the cheque had my name on it. It was given personally to *me*. In my heart I knew it was the answer to my prayer and that I should give it to church, but I recall that I did stop and think of a variety of things I could do with the money, especially as finance was tight for our family at the time. The gift was surprisingly revealing, exposing things within me that I found awkward. I talked with my wife Sam about it, who knew of my prayer, and in her no-nonsense way she said, 'Of course it's meant for the church. Thank God for it, and pass it on.' That's just what I needed to hear! And it's what I did. That experience was formative, showing me that the revealing power of money can be painful, but it's ultimately meant to lead to a deeper relationship with and reliance on God, which is a good thing.

Investing

When money does its revealing work, the good and right reaction is to respond with generosity. If we want to be released from the hold that money can have over us and use it for good, then we need to invest it, especially in the work of Christ through the local church. It's tempting to spread our giving thinly across lots of organisations, either because we want to help, or to make ourselves feel better that we're not ignoring need. But if we step back and assess, there's always much more need than we can meet, so how do we decide not just *who* we regularly give to, but *how many* people or organisations? Here's what we learned, again from our experience at St Chad's Church in Sheffield.

When I arrived in 2000 as vicar and looked at the finances and saw we were giving away less than one per cent of our income, I also noticed something fascinating: the small amount we gave was given to lots of organisations, most receiving five, ten or fifteen pounds. While it meant the church could feel good about supporting many good causes, the reality was that our giving was making little impact on any of them. So we soon stopped that and instead chose to invest in a few things well. The ones we stopped giving to didn't really miss what we'd previously given, but the ones now receiving lots were *so* grateful! Sam and I do the same: we give most of our regular giving – at least ten per cent – to the local church, and then on top we also give to a few other causes. Some of these are one-off things, which we'll address in the next chapter, but others are regular things. We've not chosen to give to too many, for we want our giving to make the greatest difference. By aiming to invest in a few things well, we've learned that less is more.[27]

Supporting

Here's what we've chosen to give to regularly, in addition to our regular giving to church. We're not suggesting you copy what we do, we're just sharing our story as an example of the kind of things that can be given to.

We support the education of two children, through World Vision Child Sponsorship, by a monthly gift. We're convinced that one of the best things we can do in life is help a child receive education. In most countries education is costly, so World Vision is one of a number of reputable organisations that supports the children of poor families in poor nations. It's an honour to give to help these children. We also give to two friends, who are serving as mission partners, supplementing their tight income. We're pleased to do this as we believe in them and in their work. We also support two charities with regular payments, as we consider their work to be important and we pray for them. These additional gifts increase our regular giving by about another five per cent. We'd love to give more, and if our income rises, we will try, recognising there are many other good causes that we don't support with money. In saying no, it doesn't mean we don't think the causes are worthy, it's just that we can't support them financially, but we will often pray for them, which we consider to be the most valuable thing we can do. Giving and prayer should go together. And if we can't give, we can certainly pray.

How Often?

There is no one set time laid down in the Bible when we're all supposed to give. Paul recommended to the Corinthian church that they give regularly. Throughout the Scriptures there's a strong link between giving and worship, and we're urged to tithe at our place of worship, so this could be done annually or monthly or weekly. The choice, I think, is ours. The most important thing is that it's regular and, we've learned, that it's assessed annually, so we can take stock, step up and continue to give cheerfully again and again.

Open-handed

One of the most influential Christian leaders of the Western church in the late twentieth century who gave regularly in this way was John Wimber. Soon after his conversion to Christ in 1963 he learned to give. He wrote about it later like this:

> I remember when I had been a Christian for about a year and clearly desiring to do something for the needy and praying for direction about it. At the time I could have been thought of as poor. Carol and I had four small babies, all under age six, and I had been out of work for several months. I did have a job at the time, but I was only bringing home $87 a week, and I was already tithing on that. As I prayed God showed me a picture of a hand, which was closed at first, but then it opened up. He then seemed to say, 'The world tells you to have a tight-fisted hand, particularly if you are in need yourself. It says you've got to cling to everything you've got. It advocates a logical and sensible economy; but that economy is not mine. I want you to see that everything is in my control and to live your life with an open hand. If you do that, I will give you ample resources both for yourself and for others.[28]

Learning

Living with an open hand, like John Wimber sought to do, raises lots of practical questions, more than we're able to fully address in this chapter. If you have tithing questions, I've found R.T. Kendall's book on the subject entitled *The Gift of Giving* to be really helpful, especially as it includes a whole chapter addressing detailed matters. Giving generously and regularly also involves planning and faith, trusting that God will help us so that the remainder will be more than enough, so we can live well and generously. If you have a fairly fixed income, you can see clearly how much is coming in and going out, so planning should be straightforward. And don't forget to give first before you spend. For many people down the ages, and especially for people in poverty whose income (even in the UK today) may be unstable or uncertain, this is harder to do. That's particularly the case if you're working on a zero-hour contract. Nevertheless, it's good to try and give a good proportion of our income away, and a greater percentage as our income rises. In the end it's not the exact percentage that matters, for God looks at the heart and the intent.[29]

When the widow of Jerusalem gave away her last two copper coins, we don't know if that was her regular giving or an occasional gift. If she lived in Jerusalem, it's likely to have been something she did regularly, but we can't be sure. Neither do we know what percentage of her income this was. All we know is that she had nothing left. She gave her all. Her giving was costly and painful. And in doing so she made herself vulnerable and dependent, both on others but especially on God. This is what happens when people in poverty give, and it's what God asks of his disciples: to learn to give in a way that's costly and makes us reliant on God's provision. Tithing, especially for those who aren't living in poverty, is a starting point in this.

As someone who receives a five-figure annual salary I am rich compared with most people in the world. When rich people like me tithe, the amount we have left is usually much more than we need to live on. More can be given. As we observe how poor people give, despite having little, we should be challenged to be even more generous. After prioritising the local church, there are other things we should be giving to, both regularly and spontaneously. The prophet Malachi called these additional things 'offerings' and distinguished them from 'tithes'.[30] These offerings point to a further aspect of giving – giving *occasionally* – which we'll explore in chapter three.

regularly

- all our resources are God's, so what we give and have left all belong to the Lord

- pray and plan your regular giving

- give the first part of your income, not your last

- aim to give at least a tithe of your income to your local church

- if you don't know how to start, just start, and pray that over time you can increase your giving

- keep giving regularly, even when it hurts

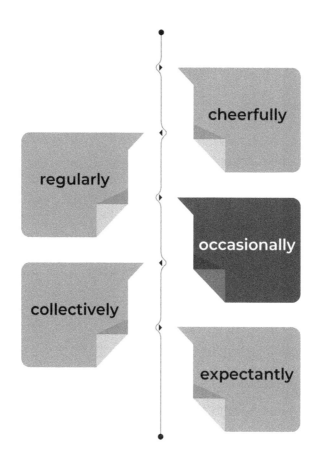

Chapter 3

- *'And do not forget to do good and to share with others, for with such sacrifices God is pleased' (Hebrews 13:16).*

- *'All they asked was that we should continue to remember the poor, the very thing I had been eager to do all along' (Galatians 2:10).*

- *'Work as hard as you can, to make all the money you can, and spend as little as you can, in order to give away all that you can' (John Wesley).*[1]

- *'Give, but give until it hurts' (Mother Teresa).*[2]

It was 1992. Sam and I had been married for a couple of years and we decided we'd like to purchase a new television set. I was especially keen on this as I enjoyed watching Manchester United on TV, but the screen on our small portable model was so small it was hard to see the ball. So we began setting aside some money and after quite a few months we were ready to start looking for a new television. Then the church we belonged to, St James' in

Doncaster, announced it was having a Gift Day soon. There were two projects they wanted to support and they invited the church to give. We loved this church community, located in one of the most deprived parishes in the country, and Sam and I wanted to contribute, so we talked about it and prayed. We didn't have any spare cash other than the money for the TV, and we didn't want to take from our regular giving to support the Gift Day, so we prayed about it for a few days and waited. When it was time for the Gift Day no additional money had come our way, so we decided to give the money we'd saved for the television. The decision was not easy for me and, if I'm totally honest, I was not a cheerful giver on that occasion! Having said that, once we'd written the cheque – as that's how you gave in those days – I felt unusually peaceful, for I knew we'd made the right decision and that it would make a difference.

That 1992 giving to our church's Gift Day wasn't a regular gift. It was a one-off. If I were to distinguish between 'tithes and offerings' using the language of Malachi 3, it was not part of our 'tithe'; rather it was an additional and occasional 'offering'. That's what this third chapter is all about: the important discipline of giving *occasionally*.

One-off

If you don't plan your giving then every time you give it's an occasional gift, but as we've seen in the previous chapter, the most effective and biblical way to give is to do so regularly, so if you've skipped chapter two, turn back and discover more about the joys and benefits of choosing to give before you spend. Having said that, there are people who give regularly and stop there. They never give occasionally, thinking that because they're giving regularly and tithe they've done enough; they've fulfilled their duty. If you are well-off and do that, search your heart. Are you tithing legalistically? Might it even be a way of avoiding generosity? This chapter urges us to push beyond tithing and instead to think generously, recognising that there's further delight and impact in giving than just giving *regularly*, for we're called to joyfully give *one-off* gifts too.

Antioch

Gift Days aren't a new thing invented in recent history. The Antioch church had one, described by Luke in Acts 11. It was sparked by Agabus, who was part of a group of travelling prophets who came to visit, and he prophesied to the Antioch church that a famine was soon to come that would impact the whole region. In today's language, they were told that a cost of living crisis was looming. The church no doubt prayed and weighed the word, and responded by taking up an offering, although no one was forced to give; it was voluntary. They then gave it all away – to the church in Jerusalem, which was around two hundred miles away. This response is telling, because when told that a cost of living crisis is coming, many people tighten their belts and hold back their giving, but the Antioch church did just the opposite! They could see they were about to experience poverty, so what did they do? They held a Gift Day, just like our church did in Doncaster, and everyone was invited to give; and then rather than keeping the offering, they gave it all away. They gave, as far as we can tell, on top of their normal regular giving. This seems like a one-off Gift Day, so it's a helpful example of giving *occasionally*.

Although we don't know the economic make-up of the members of the Antioch church, scholars think that the city was prosperous, with Josephus claiming it to be ranked third in size and wealth after Rome and Alexandria.[3] The church was growing quickly and so, just from sheer numbers, an offering from the church would probably have been significant and substantial. Despite this, Agabus' prophetic word would probably have generated anxiety in some, with many concerned for the livelihood of themselves, their family, their church and their community. It would have been so easy for a mindset of scarcity to dominate, as it has among many in our nation during the present cost of living crisis. Barnabas and Saul knew the best way to counter such a growing mindset of scarcity, and the most effective way of helping, was to give. So that's what they got the Antioch church to do. They gave.

Questions

The giving story of Antioch helps us answer three common questions about occasional giving: Why should we give occasionally? How do we give occasionally? When should we give occasionally?

Why Should We Give Occasionally?

As I write this, Turkey and Syria are suffering from a terrible humanitarian crisis after the devastating earthquake of 6th February 2023. Tens of thousands of people have lost their lives with millions left homeless. It's a desperate situation and both nations need help. My elderly mother has watched this unfold on television and she's been praying. But like many she's also given. She's given a special financial gift to support the work through the Disasters Emergency Committee, which is a collection of national aid agencies that come together to respond to emergencies overseas. She's given because she wants to bring transformation and to help.

Helping

This is what the Antioch church did, with Luke saying that they gave 'to provide help'[4] for a church almost two hundred miles away. Helping others should always be the goal of occasional giving. It's not for our benefit; it's for others. Given that the city and surrounding area of Antioch was going to be hit by the famine, it would have been tempting for the church to have kept the Gift Day for themselves, storing up provision for the coming tough season, but instead they gave it away. They wanted to support another community that they knew would struggle, and they trusted that as they did this, God would look after them.

Luke also describes a second reason for their giving that's often overlooked: it's that their giving is part of discipleship. He tells his readers that the Antioch church's giving came from 'the disciples'. His words are intentional. He could have used other words such as 'the church' or 'the people' but instead he tells us that they gave as 'disciples'. Disciples are followers of Jesus. They serve their Master, Jesus, and want to be like him. Occasional giving for the Antioch church was, it seems, part and parcel of their discipleship, and it's the same today. If we're to take our discipleship seriously, we must learn to give both regularly *and* occasionally. We discover this from lots of aspects of life, including parenthood.

Parenting
My third son Luke married his childhood sweetheart Libby in 2021. It was a wonderful day and they even invited me to preach at their wedding, which was the greatest honour. Lots of photos were taken, including one of me with my five sons at the front of church, all dressed up and looking dapper. Since the wedding a number of people have

pointed out that photo to me and they've said, 'You must be very proud of your sons.' I am. I'm truly grateful for each one. Each unique, and yet all part of our precious family. As they leave home and settle down and perhaps start their own families, what kind of lives do I want them to live? One of the most important things is that they are generous. Generous with their words and actions. Generous with their love and prayers. Generous in their churches and communities. Generous with their money. And then pass that on to the next generation too.

Where do we learn this generosity? First and foremost we learn it from our families and parents. That's why I shared some of my family experience in chapter two. While every family is different, most parents love their children and want the best for them, investing in them in so many ways. When babies arrive they're helpless; unless we feed and clothe them, change their nappies and get them to sleep, carry them and protect them, they'll die of neglect. So we start parenthood by giving, and we go on in parenthood by giving. In purely material terms, children take resources, but we don't mind, because they're our family – our beloved offspring. As they grow older, many parents will give them pocket money – normally a small amount at first and, if possible, increasing as they get older. If we do this regularly, we're modelling regular giving to them. But most parenting doesn't stop there. We give our children gifts at birthdays and Christmas. We also give occasionally in a variety of ways, from treats to school trips and much more. In short, parents give regularly *and* occasionally. It's what they do. So it is with discipleship. Disciples give regularly and occasionally. Both are important, and both are required.

How Can We Give Occasionally?

In today's digitally connected world, disasters and crises are fed to us almost instantly, as they happen. Many consider that things must be getting worse, and it's easy to feel overwhelmed with need. We know we can't help everyone, but we want to help someone. How do we do this?

Something

The church in Antioch offers great wisdom to us. They decided that together they could help some who they could foresee would struggle in the coming famine, and so people were invited to give. They gave 'as each one was able',[5] which means some would have given more and some less. Maybe a few couldn't give anything at all, although that's fairly unlikely because they saw church as a family to which they belonged, where everyone played a part, so when invited to give, each person would probably have wanted to help in some way. This means that most or all would have given something, even if it was tiny. I recommend the same today. If your church has a Gift Day and your finances are tight, don't give nothing; instead give something, for as we've been seeing in this book, when in poverty small gifts given with great love are much more powerful than we realise.

Prayerfully

There's a further thing that I expect the Antioch church did, although it's not specifically named, and that is pray. We know they did this a couple of years later, in response to another prophetic word,[6] so it's likely they did the same here. And as they prayed they received a sense of what they should do.

Most of us only have a very limited amount of money to give to occasional giving, so it's important what we give to and where. Covering these decisions in prayer is crucial for we need to ask the Lord to guide our giving so it's focused and helpful. David Watson was a well-known predecessor at The Belfrey in York who understood this, saying, 'Guidance isn't like trying to open some combination lock and thinking "If I'm lucky, I'll get it right some time." Basically, guidance is following the guide, who is Jesus.'[7] Watson knew that we seek the will of Jesus in daily prayer, as we pray the disciples' prayer: 'Your kingdom come, your will be done.'[8]

When Do We Give Occasionally?

As the Antioch church prayed and sought guidance, I expect they were prayerfully asking God all sorts of questions, including: What should we do? And what are you asking of us? These are the kind of questions we should all be asking when we come face to face with need. We know we can't respond to everything, so which do we assist? In seeking direction in this way we're trying to listen to the Holy Spirit. It was the Spirit who spoke prophetically in the first place to the Antioch church about the coming famine, so if he did that, then he would surely show the church what this meant and what they should do.[9] He will similarly guide us today.

Compassion

Sometimes we see a need in the world and we just know we need to respond. Our hearts are stirred with compassion and we want to help. While we shouldn't be led solely by our hearts, we should nevertheless listen very carefully to our emotions and be ready to respond generously, giving what we can, for this is how the Spirit sometimes guides. There's much we can learn from people in poverty here, especially when they give to a need while having so little themselves.[10] My friend Malcolm was telling me recently about a woman called Edna whom he knows, who lives on such a low income that buying an unexpected pint of milk stretches her budget. Sometimes Edna's neighbour, who is similarly poor, comes round and asks for some milk to have in her tea. When this happens Edna normally gives her the milk, because she likes her neighbour and wants to be kind to her, even though it often means that there's not enough milk for her and her family. Such is her generosity.

Invitation

There are times when we're invited by people we respect to give to a project. This might be a call from our local church or other community leaders, or perhaps there's a national or international crisis to which people are invited to give, and we feel convicted to respond, being confident about the legitimacy of the need and ability of the charitable body to use the gift well. This is what happened at Antioch, as they had their Gift Day and then entrusted the funds to trusted leaders who took it to Jerusalem.

There's one further important thing from Antioch's story that's easily missed. Luke begins his account with the following passing comment: 'The disciples were called Christians first at Antioch.'[11] This is about the year AD 46, approximately thirteen years after Jesus' death and resurrection. Before then these followers of Jesus didn't really have a designated name, although some it seems were called followers of 'the Way',[12] but now they're given the name *Christian*. This literally means 'Christ-person'. Notice that it's *this* group of people – this generous church community – that attracts the name of 'Christ'. Surely it's no mistake that the first time the word 'Christian' is ever used it describes people *giving*. We give, like the Antioch church, even when we're struggling and there's a cost of living crisis, for giving in poverty is what Christ-followers do.

Immediate

Most of us also know of times when we're confronted with an immediate need, and we must decide there and then if we're going to respond. It might involve buying a cup of tea and sandwich for someone asking for money on the street and guiding them to the nearest night shelter. It could mean topping up someone's electric meter, so they can heat their house. Or even purchasing a bus or train ticket for someone who needs to get home. Being a city-centre church in the middle of York, I know that the people of St Michael le Belfrey did this fairly often, wanting to show the loving-kindness of Jesus. Sam and I do the same, so when someone comes to our home asking for help, we'll try to make time to listen to their story and to prayerfully help where we can, which sometimes involves purchasing what they need. We don't normally give money, especially to people we don't know. That minimises exploitation or manipulation, as we've learned from bitter experience that giving money can, for some, just end up feeding an addiction. Giving practical things, as Jesus said in Matthew 25, is the best way, and an important part of the lifestyle of giving to which disciples are called. Some are able to do this more than others, or can point those in need to someone or an organisation that can help. Knowing where to direct people is particularly important, especially if you live in a deprived area; otherwise you'll often be overwhelmed by need. Much prayer and being willing to kindly but politely say 'no' as well as 'yes' is important.

Nimble

In all this, we need to be nimble and flexible, seeking attentively to walk in the Spirit. One practical way some people prepare for this is by regularly setting aside money for spontaneous or unexpected need. I have friends who, in addition to their tithe, put some money aside each month so that they can give to other things, as need arises. Sam and I do this in a small way by giving £20 per month to a Charities Aid Foundation (CAF) account in our name. As the money accumulates so a few times a year we'll give from there to a particular area of need at the time. As I am a UK tax-payer, Charities Aid Foundation claims back the tax on this from the Inland Revenue and puts it back into the account, providing us with more to give away.[13] This works well for us.

Painful

I know that some people reduce their giving to the local church so they can fund an occasional need. They're wanting to keep giving ten per cent away, but now distribute it across a number of organisations or causes. I would not recommend this. Malachi is clear that giving to God involves both tithes *and* offerings. It's not either/or, so give to both. Stay committed to tithing to your local church *and* also give to other things if you can, even though that might be difficult, painful and sacrificial. I often wonder if Matt Redman had this in mind when he penned the line, 'Though there's pain in the offering, blessed be your name.'[14] While he's probably referencing the life of sacrificial discipleship, he might also have had financial giving partly in mind, especially the giving of the poor. The widow of Jerusalem's gift of two copper coins is a case in point, for there was definitely pain in her offering, yet it was good. It can be the same for us, with our giving sometimes being demanding and sacrificial.

Obedient

Miranda, the mum I introduced earlier, told me recently that having given regularly for a while, she sensed the Holy Spirit invite her to give in addition to a new Christian ministry that was beginning. She felt the figure to give was a one-off gift of £100. This was a big ask but she began to save, and over a few months she gathered the £100. Here's how she later described what it was like to give in this way:

> I knew it was really important. It was a matter of trust and so I chose to do as God asked. It took longer than I would have liked but he helped me to fulfil that commitment. I learned

our God is faithful. He won't ask me to do what he won't enable me to do. If he asks me to give, he will provide for me to give – whatever it is.

So giving is what disciples of Jesus do, regularly and spontaneously, as we model our lives on the great giver, Jesus Christ.

Bias

Christ taught that when we give we should have a bias to the poor, and that we should especially 'give to the needy'.[15] This was particularly impressed on me one day as I read an interview with best-selling novelist John Grisham, who said, 'Jesus preached more and taught more about helping the poor and the sick and the hungry than he did about heaven and hell. Shouldn't that tell us something?'[16] It got me thinking about Christ's words that when we give to those who are 'hungry or thirsty or a stranger or needing clothes or ill or in prison' we do it for him.[17] Jesus also encouraged disciples to invite into their homes not only their families or friends, but 'the poor, the crippled, the lame, the blind'.[18] And to a rich young man he said, 'Go, sell everything you have and give to the poor.'[19] It seems the Lord notices those who are struggling or suffering, and he wants his people to support them, uphold them, being part of his means of providing for them. This emphasis on helping those who are poor is found throughout

Scripture,[20] and down the centuries preachers have often emphasised this. Jonathan Edwards, an eighteenth-century minster in Connecticut, New England, was one. He preached what's now regarded as an important sermon in 1732 on giving, entitled 'The Duty of Charity to the Poor', where he said in no uncertain terms, 'It is the absolute and indispensable duty of the people of God, to give bountifully and willingly for supplying the wants of the needy.'[21]

Many of the members of the churches I've been part of over the years have given occasionally and often spontaneously like this to people in poverty, as well as regularly serving at the local food banks. Church of England research in 2019 showed that 78 per cent of parishes were running food-banks or similar projects, and nationally 35,000 social action projects were run by local Anglican churches,[22] like the debt advice centre which The Belfrey recently established in York to help those stuck in a cycle of debt. In many communities like York, different denominations work together in this, serving charities such as Besom, who give practical things to those who have none, and Restore who provide housing for those who were previously homeless or in hostels. When I hear of all these different kinds of giving, it warms my heart. Across our nation, so many churches of different sizes and shapes and emphases care for those who are struggling. All this is part of our giving to people in poverty, because God, and his people, rightly have a bias to the poor.

This is why Christians are normally amongst the strongest voices advocating to their government that international aid to poor countries be as generous as possible. Historically the British government has been one of the few countries to commit to giving 0.7 per cent of national income to the overseas aid budget, as recommended by the United Nations. Archbishop Justin Welby reminds us that this is part of the 'political aspect to our actions'[23] and 'springs out of long campaigning by groups – Christian and otherwise – with a deep concern for global poverty'.[24] This figure was sadly reduced to 0.5 per cent during Covid lockdown and it is my hope, and that of many, that it's soon restored back to 0.7 per cent and even exceeded. In the same way that generous givers give first before they spend, so a generous nation should do the same. Giving in this way will help nations in poverty and, given that God values and honours generosity, it's short-sighted and unwise to hold back such giving.

Blessing

When Sam and I gave away the money we'd saved for the television to our church's Gift Day back in 1992, we also discovered a by-product of giving that we weren't expecting. Two weeks later someone gave us a surprise gift and it was more than enough to pay for a new television. We were delighted and thankful to God. We wondered counterfactually whether the gift to us might not have come if we'd not first given our gift to the Gift Day, but of course we'll never know. It felt like we blessed the church, and God blessed us – with a new TV! We know it doesn't always work like this, but sometimes it does – in fact, more often than we realise at the time – especially when we step out in faith and give, and particularly when we give collectively as part of a body to something important. This we'll explore in more depth in our next chapter, on giving *collectively*.

- disciples are called to give occasionally, as well as regularly

- pray when need arises, especially when you're invited to give; pay attention to your emotions and listen for the Holy Spirit's guidance

- small gifts when finances are low can make a big impact

- give with a bias to the poor

- give occasionally and spontaneously to help others

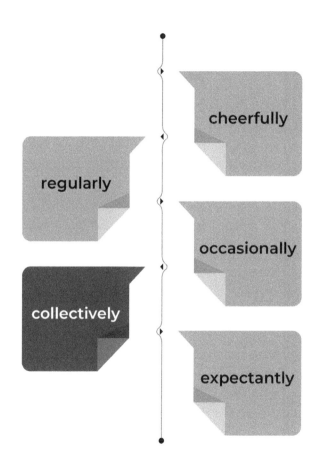

Chapter 4

collectively

- *'We want you to know about the grace that God has given the Macedonian churches. In the midst of a very severe trial, their overflowing joy and their extreme poverty welled up in rich generosity' (2 Corinthians 8:1–2).*

- *'Share with the Lord's people who are in need. Practise hospitality' (Romans 12:13).*

- *'The greatness of a community is most accurately measured by the compassionate actions of its members' (Coretta Scott King).*[1]

- *'People are motivated to give to others when they identify as part of a common community' (Adam Grant).*[2]

'I sat in my unfinished church building, wishing the still bare rafters would just fall on me.' The despairing pastor didn't know what to do. Building work on the new church had been going well, but the sudden oil crisis and devalued dollar meant his nation's economy was suddenly collapsing, with many people becoming unemployed and building costs spiralling. Maybe the God-given vision for a new building to reach their city wasn't 'God-given' after all. A few faithful friends in church decided to help by making a prayer-space, mainly for their struggling pastor, but all the minister could think about was the rising costs. One night he joined his people to pray and an old woman approached him, tears filling her eyes. She bowed and said, 'Pastor, I want to give these items to you so that you may sell them for a few pennies to help with our building fund.' He looked down and saw her holding out towards him an old rice bowl and a pair of chopsticks. He politely refused, knowing they were necessities for her. 'But Pastor, I am an old woman. I have nothing of value to give to my Lord; yet, Jesus has graciously saved me. These items are the only things in the world I possess!' she exclaimed, with tears flowing down her cheeks. 'You must let me give these to Jesus. I can place my rice on old newspapers and I can use my hands to feed myself. I know that I will die soon, so I don't want to meet Jesus without giving him something on this earth.' As she finished speaking, the pastor and all present began to weep together, and as they did so the Holy Spirit's presence filled the room and they found themselves spontaneously praying in tongues. A businessman in the back of the group was deeply moved and said, 'I want to buy that rice bowl and chopsticks for one thousand dollars!' Then, one by one, the people present began to pledge their possessions. The pastor and his wife sold their small home and gave the money to the church. And from that day in 1973 they turned a corner. The money came in; the bills were paid, and Yoido Full Gospel Church was eventually completed in Seoul, South Korea. From those difficult beginnings, stimulated by the giving of the poor, it grew into the largest church in the world and still today has nearly half a million members.[3]

Yoido Full Gospel Church's pastor was David Yonggi Cho, and as it grew so its income became huge. While they used their budget for much good in their city and nation, before he died in 2021, Cho's last ten years were marked with controversy, particularly as he was sentenced to a three-year jail sentence in 2014 for purchasing stock at an inflated price from his son's business, and for evading taxes.[4] Had money done its corrosive work, and humble beginnings been forgotten? This, then, is a cautionary tale reminding us never to become complacent about money, to have good accountability in place and to never stop learning from the generosity of poor givers.[5] Those final years of scandal, however, do not negate the reality of what happened back in 1973 when God's people came together, prayed and gave, both sacrificially and collectively, which is what this fourth chapter is all about. It's about *collective* giving: the power of togetherness, expressed in financial giving.

Togetherness

Sam and I give together. We are a couple who share finances and financial decisions. This doesn't stop her or me giving small sums without needing to ask the other. We might come across someone who is homeless and buy them some food or, as Sam did recently, give to someone we know who feels called to go abroad soon, and she gave some money to support their travel costs. But before larger sums are given we'll always talk first, for we give together as a unit, and we pray about the things and people to whom we give, asking the Lord to guide our decision-making as we seek to be generous together.

On a larger scale, this is what happens when people give to the local church. Our individual or family giving is combined with others, and together we help fund the church so it can fulfil its calling to be a worshipping and missional community. Our little may not seem that much, but when combined with the giving of others, it all adds up and is significant. It often amazes me when people tell me that they don't give because their little won't make much difference. How wrong that is, for many littles make a lot, but many think it, both inside and outside the church. That way of thinking can sometimes be challenged as leaders share vision and tell stories.

Vision

When I was vicar of The Belfrey in York I normally shared vision with our church twice a year: in January and in September. Those were times of regathering – in January after a short Christmas and New Year break, and then in September after a quiet season in August when many had been away or on holiday and church activities were reduced. They were opportune times to look back and look ahead, and to speak about plans for the coming season. In particular I talked about why we were doing what we were doing, sharing the big picture and normally rooting it in a biblical narrative. I did this partly so that people could see where we were heading, but also so people gave. I wanted the church family to give their time, energy, prayers and love to support the vision and direction of the church.

As a church leader I've always wanted our church family to go forward together, excited that we're going to help people in poverty and debt, and support refugees; eager to see people finding faith in Jesus and get baptised; pleased that we'll care for and support each other as disciples; thrilled that we'll invest in leaders, especially those who are young, and excited that we'll be starting new initiatives and planting new churches. It's from this place of vision – starting with the why[6] – that I would ask people to give, because people give to vision. Usually in January I'd invite everyone to look at their income and renew their financial giving for the coming year – both their giving to us, and to other matters. Often we'd ask people to prayerfully complete a pledge form, which enabled them to plan their giving (see chapter two) and helped the church leadership have an idea of what the income might look like in the coming year. When casting vision in this way I was wanting people to see that their giving would help support the wider vision, and that *together* our collective giving could make a genuine difference in our city and beyond.

Stories

I also discovered that telling stories was another way of inspiring people, which had the bi-product of releasing giving in a variety of ways. As we tell stories of people who've volunteered and helped others, often people want to give time to volunteering. As we tell stories of people finding faith in Jesus and getting baptised, so some will commit to sharing their faith more or supporting the next Alpha course. As we tell stories about revitalised churches, some will want to give themselves to praying for more future plants, for a good team to come together for the next one, and for us to fill up again so we can do it again. Some will simply want to give financially to some or all of these things. It's all linked up. Sharing vision and telling stories raise faith and expectation, causing people to want to give.

Leaders, then, have a crucial role in encouraging everyone to see that their giving is like a jigsaw piece that's an important part of the whole puzzle. As we know, a jigsaw with even just one piece missing is *so* frustrating! It's annoying, not only because it doesn't look right but also because it's just incomplete. So it is with our giving. It's only as we all give collectively that the full benefit is realised.

Macedonia

The church that stands out in the Bible as a great example of a community who all gave collectively is the church in the province of Macedonia. This group of local churches was begun by Paul on his Second Missionary Journey and referenced in Acts 16 and 17, and they include Philippi, Thessalonica and Berea. Paul describes their giving in 2 Corinthians 8:2, saying, 'In the midst of a very severe trial, their overwhelming joy and their extreme poverty welled up in rich generosity.' Dig deep into these verses and we see three important things about the Macedonian's collective giving.

i) They gave out of deep poverty

When I was a teenager, a friend and I spent a weekend with a family who lived in a council flat in inner-city Tottenham in London, while we and four others undertook a school research project in the area. They welcomed us into their home and showed us kindness, giving us somewhere to sleep and a base to work from. There wasn't much on the kitchen shelves: a few tins and some pasta, which they shared with us as we ate together. They said we could help ourselves to food from the fridge if we needed to. So later I opened the fridge door to grab a snack, and what

I saw shocked me. There was some butter and a jar of ketchup and nothing else. That was all. I'd never seen such an empty fridge. It was then that it dawned on me that maybe this family were living on the edge of poverty, and yet they were showing us great kindness in opening their home to us and sharing their precious food with us. For the first time in my life my eyes were opened to the giving of people in poverty.

The widow of Jerusalem, who we're considering in every chapter of this book, was a poor person who gave generously to a collective offering. That's easily missed. She added her small contribution to the much larger offering, and Jesus honoured her heart and her generous intent. When Jesus said that she gave 'more' than the others I've often wondered what 'more' Jesus was talking about. Clearly her giving was *more costly* – and that's probably what Jesus meant. But maybe it involved *more love*. Certainly it was a *more vulnerable* offering, making her *more dependent*. I also wonder whether it was *more catalytical*, with its sacrificial nature releasing *more kingdom energy* than the other less costly gifts. I can't prove that, but that's my hunch. That's why I loved watching my children give when they were young. We would give them £1 pocket money each per week, and they would come to church and put ten pence in the church collection each week, as it got passed round. This was costly for them, and

I often wondered if it was part of the 'more' that Christ observed and loved and blessed as he looked on at the offerings given in our church.

The giving of the church community in Macedonia was also costly, because they were poor. In fact Paul describes them not just as poor but living 'in extreme poverty', and yet they still chose to support his missionary work and that of his associates. Like the family in Tottenham and the widow of Jerusalem, they're another example of generous poor people. But what's interesting about the Macedonians is that they gave *collectively*, together as God's people.

One person who I like to think valued the Macedonian church was George Porter, the brother of my great-grandfather, William. After the premature death of their father in the early 1860s the two boys, with their mother, Anne, found themselves living in poverty and having to do all they could to make ends meet to bring money into the household. It was the height of the Industrial Revolution so the children began making nails for carpenters and blacksmiths from the back yard of their home in Skelmanthorpe, near Huddersfield in West Yorkshire. It was here they learnt basic manufacturing and business skills which, over time, helped them to become astute in business. On reaching their twenties William moved to the town of Doncaster and married Arabella, the daughter of a Methodist minister; one of their children, Luther, was my grandfather. George, however, moved to the town of Barnsley and married Lena, the daughter of a loom manufacturer, and went into her family business. He also helped Anne, his mother, set up a high-street shop on Eldon Street in Barnsley. It was called A. Porter & Sons and began as a china and crockery shop, which developed into a successful high-class general store,[7] with Anne still honoured today in Barnsley as a pioneering early female business leader in the town. All the family had a strong faith in Christ and in my library I have George's copy of an 1850 commentary on 2 Corinthians, entitled *Notes on the Second Epistle to the Corinthians and the Epistle to the Galatians* by Albert Barnes. Stamped with 'G. Porter' on the inside, it's likely that 2 Corinthians was one of the books in the Bible that influenced George as he sought to live as a Christian entrepreneurial businessman in Barnsley. Here are Barnes' notes about chapter eight of 2 Corinthians, on the giving of the Macedonian church, which would have been read by George:

> *v2. How that, in a great trial of affliction.* When it might be supposed they were unable to give; when money would suppose they needed the aid of others; or when it might be supposed their minds would be wholly engrossed with their own concerns . . .
>
> *And their deep poverty.* Their very low estate of poverty was made to contribute liberally to the wants of others. It is implied here, (1,) that they were very poor . . . (2,) That

notwithstanding this they were enabled to make a liberal contribution – a fact demonstrating that a people *can* do much even when poor, if all feel disposed to do it . . .[8]

George would have understood that while the Macedonians had little, they still gave, and their collective giving added up and was greatly impactful. George knew what it was to live in poverty, and later to live in affluence. Was he similarly generous in his giving? I don't know. But I do know he joined and supported Pitt Street Methodist Church in Barnsley, the church that in the previous generation had sent out the missionary Hudson Taylor to China, and so I hope he became caught up in the generosity of that church, and together with his church family learned the art of giving. For Barnes is right: even if people are poor, when a community gives it can be highly significant if 'all' do it together.

ii) *Their giving overflowed*

As the poor Macedonians poured out their giving so it spilled out beyond them and had a great impact. That's why the Greek word 'overflow' and its derivatives are used a number of times in this passage describing the Macedonians. A literal translation of verse two could read, 'In much trial of tribulation, their overflowing joy and their deep water of poverty overflowed into their rich generosity.'[9] Paul intentionally uses liquid language here, describing their poverty as extreme, like deep water (Greek: *bathous* from which we get the English words 'bath' and 'bathe'). Despite being poor the Macedonians had such an abundance of joy in Christ that it overflowed, spilling out no doubt in a variety of expressions, and especially in wanting to give. They were *so* thrilled and excited about giving, and so should we be. Indeed they're a great example of cheerful givers (see chapter one)! And the result of it all was a further overflow of rich generosity.

Here in Macedonia we have a clash of worlds: the world of scarcity meets the world of abundance, and the world of abundance triumphs. How? Through their generous giving. This is particularly the case because of the collective nature of their giving. It wasn't just one or two people who gave, but lots. Together they created a tidal wave of overflowing generosity that hit Paul like a tsunami!

iii) They gave beyond their ability

One reason for this is that the Macedonian Christians didn't just give minimally; instead they gave 'as much as they were able, and even beyond their ability'.[10] We don't know why or how they did this, but maybe it's because when we give *with others*, we can give more than we think. When we see others giving who don't have much, we realise we can do the same. It looks like in doing this some probably overstretched themselves, perhaps giving all they had like the widow of Jerusalem in Luke 21. As a church leader who wants to encourage wise steward- ship, this is not something I would ever suggest someone should do, but I am aware that sometimes God asks peo- ple to do this. They then have to trust that God will look after them.[11] Paul sees this as a natural outworking of their discipleship, saying that '[having given] themselves first of all to the Lord, and then by the will of God also to us'.[12] So he picks up two forms of giving. First there is a giving to God – a consecration of lives laid down, and second there is a giving of money. And they shared in both *together*, as a community, and it was powerful.

Me

The *together* part of giving is so easily lost on Western peo- ple today. As people brought up in a culture of individual- ism, we read most stories and texts of the Bible through a 'me' lens, and we forget that most of the time 'you' is in the plural. This is particularly the case when money and giving are addressed. Giving together is so much better. When we do this we're adding to other people's gifts and making them bigger and more impactful. We're not out to make a name for ourselves by our giving, as some philanthropists do. No, we're giving humbly, with others, and if there is any praise or thanks to be given, it's for the collective body and for Christ himself, who leads us. Giving like this, together in community, reminds us that we're part of something bigger and greater than me – a family. The body of Christ. And this is good. Really good.

Others

If giving really *is* good, bringing joy not just to the recipient but to the body through whom it comes, and if it truly *is* central to the life and work of God's kingdom, then we must encourage each other in our giving. We must 'spur one another on towards love and good deeds'.[13] Eugene H. Peterson agrees and expresses it like this: 'The primary concern of what we are doing together in this Christian life is to help one another get in on the whole thing, a full life, not leaving anything out, not settling for too little.'[14] So my giving doesn't just help the recipient but also helps the giving of others too! How good is that?!

Team

This doesn't mean that giving is easy. In fact for many it's a battle, which is a further reason why it's good to give in community, along with others. I was reminded of this by the simple illustration of George Hunter, who said, 'A zoologist once informed me that a tiger will defeat a lion in battle, but five lions will defeat five tigers because the lions fight as a team and the tigers do not.'[15] That's why we give in teams, together as God's people.

You'd think team giving is easier when you're rich, compared to when you're poor, but surveys show the opposite is the case. Surveys consistently show that churches in poorer communities often give more than those in wealthier neighbourhoods, with most poor Christ-followers giving proportionately more than richer ones.[16] For those of us in the affluent West today, we again need to learn from the generous giving of the poor, and from communities like the Macedonian church. They gave as part of their discipleship, as part of their communal following of Jesus, and we need to do the same, heeding the words of David Watson, who said:

> Discipleship is never easy; often there may be pain and tears, and frequently we shall have to re-think our values and ambitions as we seek seriously to follow Christ. But we are not called to face this challenge on our own. Alongside the inward power of the Holy Spirit, God wants us to experience the encouraging, supportive love of other disciples of Jesus. It is in the strength of our relationships together in Christ that we can win the battles against the power of darkness and help one another to fulfil the task that God has given us.[17]

This means we need to talk more about giving, and not be embarrassed about it. We need to encourage each other in our giving without forcing anyone to give. And we must stretch ourselves in our giving, learning from the generosity of people in poverty.

Saving

'This fund has changed my life' was the message I heard time and again when in 2017 I visited villages in Rwanda, as I heard about the programme that Tearfund was encouraging. One woman told me, 'On my own I would never be able to afford a sewing machine but the community fund helped me.' Another used it to buy chickens to start a simple poultry business. It was essentially a micro-finance loan programme, where people gave a small amount centrally to a fund, from which they could apply for a loan to help start a business, or pay for education, or meet other needs. People gave a very small amount, but by giving collectively and prayerfully the fund grew to a size to be able to make a significant contribution in helping lift people out of poverty, one family at a time.[18] A number of charitable organisations encourage this, often giving seed money to help get the programme started, recognising the transformative value of saving *together* in this way. Recent research by Tearfund evidences this, showing that through this local community approach, every £1 given produces £28 of social value.[19] Not only that, it also creates unity and social cohesion in villages, as people realise that they're helping each other, and doing it together.

Unity

If we stand back and think about it, much giving is corporate, even if we don't realise it. For example, when we give to an emergency appeal from a relief agency, we're joining with many others, adding our contribution to theirs. When we give to our diocese, we're giving alongside many other churches. Even when we pay our taxes, we're joining with others in our shared contribution to the good of our nation, which includes giving a small contribution to other nations too. This is how it should be. Giving should be a mark of unity and solidarity.

We've been learning about collective giving in this chapter from the poor church(es) in Macedonia, named in 2 Corinthians 8. As Paul concludes his comments on their giving, he makes a simple statement to his listeners in Corinth, which continues to be a sound message for us all: 'See that you also excel in this grace of giving.'[20] We're *all* to learn from the Macedonians, and in doing so increasingly excel in giving. Giving is a grace; a gift. It's given to us by Christ, the great gift-giver, so that we can give not just once, but again and again. That's how grace works, as we'll explore in our final chapter where we consider what it means to give *expectantly*.

- collective giving is inspired by vision-casting and story-telling

- with others we can give more than we think

- giving is hard; it's easier when we give together, encouraging each other

- giving is a battle, so fight together by giving together

- give joyfully with overflowing generosity

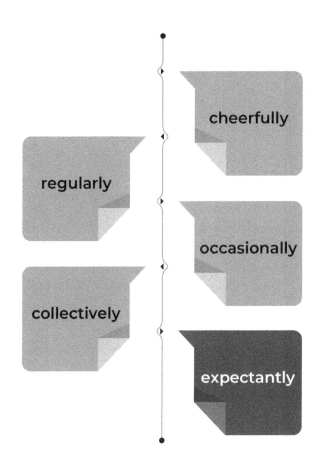

Chapter 5

- *'Give, and it will be given to you. A good measure, pressed down, shaken together and running over, will be poured into your lap' (Luke 6:38).*

- *God 'is able to do immeasurably more than all we ask or imagine' (Ephesians 3:20).*

- *'Generosity is paradoxical. Those who give their resources away, receive back in return' (Christian Smith and Hilary Davidson, The Paradox of Generosity, Oxford University Press 2014).[1]*

- *'What we give we gain' (Justin Welby).[2]*

George Müller woke up one morning, aware that provisions at his orphanage in Bristol, England, were virtually depleted, but trusting the Lord would provide as they continued to give love, care and shelter to many orphans in the city. That morning Abigail Townsend Luffe was present with her father, who often assisted Müller at the Ashley Down orphanage. Abigail later recalled what happened that mid-nineteenth-century day. Müller led her into the long dining room set ready for breakfast but without food. He prayed, 'Dear Father, we thank Thee for what Thou art going to give us to eat.' A few moments later there was a knock at the door; it was a baker who'd been up early, unable to sleep because he was convinced God wanted him to bake bread for the orphanage. 'Children,' Müller said, 'we not only have bread, but *fresh* bread.' Almost immediately there was a second knock. It was a milkman; the milk cart had broken down outside the orphanage, and he offered the milk to the children, completing their meal. This is how Müller lived, praying and trusting that as he and his team generously gave themselves to the work of God, so the Lord would provide, again and again. In his autobiography he expressed it in this way: 'After the Lord has tried our faith, He, in the love of His heart, gives us an abundance. For the glory of His name and for trial of our faith, He allows us to be poor and then graciously supplies our needs.'[3]

Jesus said that when we give generously, God also gives back liberally to us.[4] The psalmist penned that 'good will come to those who are generous and lend freely'.[5] The apostle Paul agreed, saying to the church in Corinth that having given, the Lord 'who supplies seed to the sower and bread for food will also supply and increase your store of seed and will enlarge the harvest of your righteousness' so they can continue to 'be generous on every occasion'.[6] These are remarkable statements. They imply that when we give we should do so with the expectation that not only will the recipient be helped, but that God will look after us, the givers. He will provide. At least he will ensure we can survive, but very often it's much more than that. Often he gives back what we've given, or sometimes even more. Such is the kindness and generosity of God. This means we can trust him and give *expectantly*, which is the theme of this final chapter of *The Art of Giving*.

Benefits

Giving away is highly counter-intuitive. Human beings instinctively think that if we give we have less. As we saw in chapter one, this is a scarcity mindset, where we assume that there's only a limited amount of resource, so when we give money, the supply has decreased. But we don't think that way about love. When we give love, we don't have less afterwards. People with a number of children don't love each one less than those with only a few. Love expands! And Christians don't think in a diminishing way about prayer. When we intercede and ask God for things in prayer, we don't assume that we should stop after a few prayers because we've used up all our prayer allowance. No, we call out to God for lots of things and people and situations. So what if we transferred that thinking to all the resources in God's kingdom, including our giving? Justin Welby encourages this, inviting us to consider financial giving through the lens of systems thinking. Rather than assuming that when I give 'I lose', which reflects a *closed system* mentality, we can think 'abundance and generosity', which implies an *open system* in which 'the creative power of God is ever active, so that what we give we gain',[7] Research seems to agree with this 'divine economics' approach, showing that giving not only facilitates the common good but also that those who give financially receive back in all sorts of ways. Here are five possible ways:[8]

1. **Giving makes us happier**. A 2008 study by Michael Norton of Harvard Business School found that giving money to someone else lifted participants' happiness more than spending it on themselves, despite participants' prediction that spending on themselves would make them happier.[9]

2. **Giving makes us healthier**. It can help those with chronic illnesses, like multiple sclerosis and HIV, it can lower blood pressure and even lower the risk of dying.[10]

3. **Giving promotes neighbourliness**. Giving money stimulates social interaction and provides people with purpose and helps them feel part of a community.[11]

4. **Giving evokes gratitude**. Giving often produces gratitude, not just in the recipient but also in the giver, and gratitude is integral to happiness and health. Many studies have shown how it's good for us and others, helping us thankfully perceive a world of resources rather than scarcity.[12]

5. **Giving can be infectious**. Organisational psychologist and author Adam Grant recognises this, saying that 'giving, especially when it's distinctive and consistent, establishes a pattern that shifts other people's reciprocity styles within a group'. 'It turns out,' says Grant, 'that giving can be contagious.'[13]

But can giving money also be financially beneficial? Are we better off by giving? Some are reluctant to even suggest this, recognising that when we give, our bank balances normally go down and not up! Also, many Christian leaders, like me, are rightly wary of promoting the *prosperity gospel*, which urges people to give in order to get rich. Such a motive is patently distorted and wrong, and needs exposing as selfish and sinful. However, the plain reading of Scriptures such as Luke 6:38 and 2 Corinthians 9:10 suggest there *are* financial benefits to giving. And there is much empirical evidence to agree. Adam Grant's conclusion, after his detailed and long-view study on the subject, is this: 'People who give more go on to earn more . . . Research shows that giving can boost happiness and meaning, motivating people to work harder and earn more money.'[14] Smith and Davidson also agree, concluding in their important Oxford University Press monograph entitled *The Paradox of Generosity*, that:

Generosity is paradoxical. Those who give their resources away, receive back in turn. In offering time, money, and energy in service of others' well-being, we enhance our own well-being as well. In letting go of some of what we own for the good of others, we better secure our own lives, too. This paradox of generosity is a sociological fact, confirmed by evidence drawn from quantitative surveys and qualitative interviews.[15] (*Christian Smith and Hilary Davidson, The Paradox of Generosity, Oxford University Press 2014*)

Might these be signs that 'the floodgates of heaven' are open, in response to generous giving, as Malachi suggests?[16] Could they be the 'rewards' that Jesus talks about in the Sermon on the Mount?[17] I think so. It seems that as we give, God gives back. Occasionally he does this immediately. Mostly it's over a period of time, and so it's not always easy or possible to adequately quantify. Maybe the Lord enables the washing machine to break down less often; the car service to be cheaper; the fruit crop to be more abundant; surprise gifts to come more often.[18] Maybe. But whether this is how it works or not, what is clear is that it's not so we get rich. No, it's so we can be generous again! It's so we can live and give. As Paul says in 2 Corinthians 9:10, it's so we have bread to eat (for us) and seed to sow (to give to others).[19] That's the difference between the *prosperity gospel* and the *generosity gospel*.[20] The prosperity gospel is primarily for my benefit while the generosity gospel is to benefit others.

Motivation

It's quite common to hear people say that this kind of generosity is about giving with no intent to get anything back. Pope Benedict XVI advocated this at the end of his encyclical *Caritas in Veritae.*[21] This is quite correct. We don't give to gain from others. We mustn't give for the purpose of receiving – either from people or from God. No, as we've seen, we give to see transformation and so even if we gain nothing back materially, it's still worth doing. But . . . (and this is an important 'but') . . . the reality is that we *will* receive something back, for Jesus said so. The benefit might be material, or psychological, or both, or come in some other form. But we will. It's like when we give love, we normally receive love back. It's the way God has made the world! It's rather like saying, as I sometimes do, that we should worship with no desire to get anything out of it, because worship is primarily for *God's* benefit. This is true. We worship God because he deserves our praise. And yet when we worship, we receive. We receive forgiveness, peace and perspective – and much more too.[22] We just do. The Scriptures are explicit about this, saying that when we draw near to God, he draws near to us.[23] It's just what happens! Similarly, it's good to give with no intent to receive but, in saying that, we mustn't deny the fact that we *will* receive. This is because we can't outgive God.[24] It sounds corny, but it's true. God is richly generous! Author and church leader Mark Batterson expresses it like this:

> I believe in the law of measures. If you give big, God will bless big. That certainly doesn't mean you can play God like a slot machine, but if you give for the right reasons, I'm convinced of this: *You'll never outgive God.* It's not possible because God has promised that in the grand scheme of eternity, He will always give back more than you gave up.[25]

Ephesus

One New Testament church that was taught this paradox of generosity was the Ephesian church. They're a good example for this chapter's theme of *expectant* giving. Paul invested significant time in this church, successfully establishing it as a key mission and church-planting base for the region. We read about them in Acts 19. Formed in the early AD 50s[26] in the context of people being filled with the Holy Spirit and experiencing extraordinary miracles and deliverances, the church was later led by a young pastor called Timothy, with Paul's two letters to Timothy providing fatherly guidance on many aspects of church leadership.

Paul's love for this Ephesian church is evident in Acts 20, in his emotional farewell speech to the Ephesian elders, probably delivered around AD 57.[27] Knowing he'll never see them again, it's rich in practical advice and emotive in content, ending with Luke describing a scene of much hugging and weeping. Over the years I've heard a number of talks on this passage, and most emphasise the way Paul has poured his life and teaching into these people, and how he now urges them to keep watch and stay faithful. However, what is sometimes missed, or only covered briefly, is how Paul closes his speech. Most speechmakers know that how you conclude is crucial. In fact many orators will build to a climax, with some saving their most important take-away for the end. So how does Paul end? The answer is that he finishes by talking about giving. His final words are about money, saying that he took care while with them not to benefit financially, and he urges them not to seek material riches but instead that they 'must help the weak, remembering the words the Lord Jesus himself said: "It is more blessed to give than to receive."'[28]

Paul could have said many things to them in his parting words. It fascinates me that he tells them to *keep giving*, like him. The motive for this is not for financial gain but for the expansion of the gospel, and caring for the poor and weak. This is wisdom indeed, for he knows that it's through giving that transformation comes, with the by-product being that they too will be blessed, so they can keep giving. This is the expectation of giving.

After saying goodbye to the Ephesian elders Paul wrote a letter to this church in Ephesus;[29] we know it today simply as *Ephesians*. At the heart of this letter is a most beautiful prayer of Paul, which he prays over them. Captivated by the 'glorious riches' of the Father and the power that comes 'through his Spirit',[30] he focuses on the wonder of the indwelling Christ, and gets lost in prose as he declares his prayer for them:

> I pray that you, being rooted and established in love, may have power together with all the Lord's holy people, to grasp how wide and long and high and deep is the love of Christ, and to know this love that surpasses knowledge – that you may be filled to the measure of all the fulness of God.[31]

These are heartening words, rich in gracious good intent. He wants the Ephesians to know that the God revealed in Christ is superbly generous, so they are liberally filled to overflowing with his love. But what is this love for? Is it just so they enjoy the presence of Jesus? No. It's given so they can live lives of giving, which is what the remaining chapters of the letter to the Ephesians are all about: the grace of God expressed in leadership and life (chapter four), and in words, relationships and prayers (chapters five and six). Unsurprisingly, the last verse of the letter says, 'Grace to all'.[32] Given John Stott's helpful reminder that grace 'is another word for generosity',[33] this means Paul closes this letter by declaring, 'Generosity to all.' That's why it's good to see that the Ephesians went on to give generously, giving away not just money but people whom they sent out to plant many churches. In giving like this, they started a powerful movement of church planting that impacted not just their region but the future trajectory of church history.[34]

Largeness

This inspiring church in Ephesus learned not to limit their giving, discovering instead that the nature of God and his kingdom is vast and expansive. Perhaps word-smith Eugene H. Peterson was hinting at this wideness in the mercy and grace of God when he wrote about the joy of 'living into the largeness of God'.[35] There is indeed a grandness to the generosity of God, which the Spirit of Jesus invites us to playfully explore. This echoes something of my experience of the churches I have led, both in Sheffield and more recently at The Belfrey in York.

In the summer of 2019 Ben Doolan, one of the clergy from The Belfrey, moved ninety miles north to Newcastle to help revitalise St Thomas' Church, which had a congregation of about ten. We sent with Ben a great team of thirty-two adults and three children. While we were sad to see them go, we knew the Lord had called them to this venture, and we were excited to watch how things would go and grow.

Since arriving and re-booting the church, they've not only walked through the intricacies of Covid-19 but also renovated their building, and in a relatively short space of time Sunday attendance at St Thomas' is over 300 and growing. Before then we'd been involved in a number of planting-type ventures, but this plant seemed especially significant, both for the church being planted and also for us, as it felt like there were key lessons to be learned as we planned to regularly and healthily plant into the future.

When the team left for Newcastle it left a gap in the sending church in York. I trusted that the Lord would refill the gap, but looking back now I was probably a little more apprehensive than I realised, concerned that we'd be alright and be able to do it again. In September, two months after we'd sent out the team to Newcastle, we had our next monthly welcome lunch for new people at our vicarage, having paused the August one for holidays. This lunch is for newcomers who've started coming to our church and want to find out more. Not everyone who comes stays with us, but the majority do. Before lunch began I enquired how many newcomers we had coming that day, and was told 'thirty-two adults and three children'. I caught my breath and smiled, for those were exactly the same numbers we'd recently sent to Newcastle. I felt like the Lord was arresting my attention and saying, 'Look, I can fill you back up straight away if I want to. So don't worry.'

In January 2022, after Covid lockdown, we planted our next church. The Belfrey plan to do another in 2024, and another in 2026, as the church is now on a rolling programme with the diocese to give away people every two years to this, believing that God will honour their giving, so they can give again, and again.

The Lord has been very generous to The Belfrey over the last few years, especially giving a number of large financial gifts to add to the regular giving that the church family generously gives. They've been learning to use these gifts well, and not to hold on tightly to them. So a Northern Church Planting Fund has been established to help churches be planted or revitalised in our region, and a Love York Post-Pandemic Fund for social action in the locality, as well as financing more outreach staff to serve the city. Incredibly, generous gifts have also been given to Impact – the church's building project – which is all about creating a flexible base for worship and mission, in preparation for the long-term ministry they're called to going ahead. As they've been learning about stewarding and giving money, so the Lord has also been teaching the people at The Belfrey about giving people again and again, for the task of church planting. They know this will stretch them, but they're trusting that as they seek to be a generous church so the Lord will be generous to them. All this has been captured in the word *overflow.*

Overflow was the word of the year for the church in 2018. It encapsulated what I, as vicar, felt the Holy Spirit had impressed on me in 2017 as I prayed and pondered about the year ahead. Some people and prophetic messages had also confirmed this, which gave me confidence as we went into the new year and prepared for the church plant in Newcastle. The message was simple: as God pours in, so we must pour out. He is not short of resources to give, or love to share. We're not to hold on to what the Spirit brings but let it go. As we do this, so God will keep pouring. I spoke for three consecutive weeks about this in January 2018 and then later wrote in more detail about it in a book entitled *Overflow*.[36] Just before I spoke in the January, a part broke in the upstairs toilet in our home, which meant that the overflow mechanism was permanently engaged, so when I woke up in the night or in the morning when everything was quiet, all I could hear was the sound of overflow. This was my experience throughout the time I preached on the subject, as it took three weeks for the plumbers to come and replace the broken part. I took note that it was fixed immediately after I preached the last sermon! Later in the year, in September, I chose to speak once more on the theme of overflow. Early on the Sunday morning, on the very day I was due to speak, I woke up in the night and could hear a familiar sound in the distance. I got up to investigate. Our other bathroom toilet had just broken in exactly the same place, releasing again the sound of overflow. I laughed and thanked the Lord for his sense of humour, for it seemed that whenever I was preaching on overflow there were signs following – reminding me that he really is the God of overflow!

This understanding of God being large and in charge – a great and generous God of overflow who keeps pouring out[37] – encourages us to be a people who, like him, over-flow with generosity. It reflects Jesus' radical teaching in Luke 6:38:

> Give, and it will be given to you. A good measure, pressed down, shaken together and running over, will be poured into your lap. For with the measure you use, it will be measured to you.

Gateway

As we've seen, giving money is central to this overflowing life of discipleship. It's not by any means the only form of giving, but it's basic to the lifestyle of generosity to which we're called. Indeed if we can't give financially, even if we have very little, then we will find it hard to give in other ways. This has been my experience, and that of the churches I've led, and we see it in the five churches mentioned in this book too: Philippi (chapter one); Corinth (chapter two); Antioch (chapter three); Macedonian churches (chapter four) and Ephesus (chapter five). We observe that giving money unlocks our hearts to other forms of giving.[38] This is especially true when times are tough, which is why we need to keep learning from the generosity of people in poverty, like the widow of Jerusalem, who so helpfully models what costly financial giving looks like.

Financial giving seems to be a gateway gift for people, releasing other forms of giving in them and producing lots of good to others. Research shows this, that giving money changes our brains[39] so that givers begin to 'see potential all around them'[40] and that those who give financially also give their time, energy and resources in other ways, for example through volunteering, caring, as well as speaking words of encouragement.[41] Often as we give money, new areas of responsibility open up for us too. Indeed Jesus said this would be the case, when he said:

> Whoever can be trusted with very little can also be trusted with much, and whoever is dishonest with very little will also be dishonest with much. So if you have not been trustworthy in handling worldly wealth, who will trust you with true riches?[42]

Risk

Having said all this, what happens if we give and don't fill up, and resources run out? What if we've generously given and prayed with passion, and yet we still lack? These are the all too real questions sometimes asked by starving communities in parts of Africa, who are short of food and water. They're also asked by persecuted communities in Asia whose churches have been burned and whose friends and colleagues have been martyred. I've met people asking these questions as I've travelled, and more recently as I've studied with a cohort of international pastors and church planters, some of whom have given their time and love and material resources, but it seems like God has not always answered their prayers and they don't always see overflow. Why?

To properly answer such a question would require a book in its own right on the theology of suffering, and so I am reluctant to offer superficial answers. However, *not* to say anything would be remiss, given the message of this book about giving. So despite there being no easy answers, here are a few thoughts that may assist those who seek to live generously and yet find themselves in financial straits.

1. **Ask for help**. There's nothing wrong with asking for help – not just from God in prayer, but also from family, friends, neighbours, churches, charities, town councils or governments. No caring person or body wants to see another suffering, and it may be that one of these bodies may be the provider of the resources that you need and are praying for. Also, churches have a mandate from

God to listen to the cry of the poor and oppressed,[43] so if there are Christians or churches, particularly nearby, who have resources to help, they must.[44] Not to do so is to be disobedient. Maybe one reason some people are starving and poor today is that God's church is not stepping up sufficiently and giving like we should. This is a challenge to every believer, including me. May the Lord have mercy, and help us to do all we can.

2. **Find strength in Scripture**. Many of the prayers in the book of Psalms are cries of desperation, calling for help and sometimes asking God why prayers seem unanswered.[45] The fact that these prayers are included in the Bible, God's Word, shows there's no shame in feeling this way or praying like this. God understands, so don't stop. Of course some of the recorded prayers prayed in the Bible take time to be answered, and so a long-view must be taken. I recognise that this is often hard and harrowing, especially when it's your friend who's suffering or your child who's starving, and time is short.

3. **Use what you have**. There are many stories in the Bible where someone thinks they're at the end of their tether and have nothing, but when they take stock they're surprised with the resources they already have in front of them. The story of the widow in 2 Kings 4 is a case in point. She has no money and her sons are about to be taken into slavery. Elisha asks her what she has in her house, and she replies, 'Nothing.' Then after some

thought she says, 'except a little olive oil', and it's that small resource of oil that the Lord then uses to release provision.[46] The Christian aid agency Tearfund have been using this approach for a number of years through their Church and Community Mobilisation programme,[47] as I discovered in Rwanda. It begins by encouraging people to see and then prayerfully use the resources they already have and watch what the Lord does. Some of the outcomes are truly amazing.

4. **Stay generous**. Even if you have virtually nothing, do your best to share what you have. Not only will it help those around you, but God will honour the sharing and the sacrifice. Richard Wurmbrand discovered this when a prisoner in communist Eastern Europe in the 1970s and '80s. His crime was simply that he was a Christian and church leader. On one occasion when in prison he received an illicit gift of two lumps of sugar, but he decided not to eat them, instead passing them on to someone in a worse state. Then he discovered they'd not eaten them either. In fact the lumps lasted for two years, passed on from one prisoner to another. As they were given away, again and again, so they became known to many prisoners as a symbol, not only of self-sacrifice but also of hope.[48] Such is the power of generous, costly giving.

5. **Trust God**. When times are hard, trusting anyone can be incredibly difficult, especially God. As we take a

long-term view, this trusting might mean that sadly some don't make it and they die – perhaps of starvation or illness. Many have walked this road of intense suffering in days gone by, paying the ultimate giving sacrifice: giving up their very lives.[49] When this happens due to lack of resources, this is unthinkably tragic, especially for those left behind. At such times what can we do but sit with the grieving, as we 'mourn with those who mourn'?[50] Those who have witnessed such things know they point to the fragility of life and cause us to long for heaven, where there will be no more scarcity. At such dark times, we need the comfort of the Holy Spirit and the supportive kindness of God's people.[51] While it's understandable that some may blame God in bleak days, it's better and wiser to throw ourselves onto God. The history of God's people down the ages shows that those who do this and put their trust in him, often find themselves surprisingly carried and remarkably sustained, even as they walk through the valley of the shadow of death.

Trust

Eighteenth-century minister Jonathan Edwards understood this. Although not poor, Edwards knew about tragedy, with much death around him in his parish, his wife often suffering depression, and after a long and fruitful ministry he was even sacked by his church. But this did not stop him believing and preaching on the benefits of giving, which he held to all his life. He believed that God blesses the giver so they can give again, saying, 'What is bestowed in charity is lent to the Lord, and he repays with great increase . . . God has told us that this is the way to have his blessing attending our affairs.' Edwards taught that giving 'doth not tend to poverty, but to the contrary. It is not the way to diminish our substance, but to increase it. All the difficulty in this matter is in trusting God.'[52]

As Sam and I look back on our lives so far, we have not always trusted God very well in our giving, but we have tried. We recognise that God has looked on our hearts and blessed our desire to be generous. In no way are we experts at giving, and we're sure there are many who are much more generous in their giving than us, but nevertheless it seems that the Lord has looked after us and provided for us as we've sought to live generously. In fact he's sometimes done this in miraculous ways, enabling us to give again. Even now as I write this, with bills increasing and disposable income becoming smaller each month, we're aiming not to reduce our financial giving, and the Lord has continued to look after us. We are grateful for the rewards of giving, so we can do it again and again.

Xander discovered something of these rewards a few years ago. He described to me how he'd just been paid in cash and so had two weeks' pay with him as he came into church. As he entered the building he saw someone he knew and sensed the Holy Spirit tell him to give this person all the money he had with him. He had a conversation with God about this over a few minutes, to be sure this is what he was being asked to do. Convinced it was, Xander gave the money, asking the Lord to look after him as he would now be short. Two days later a Christian friend called him and said that while praying they felt they should give him a particular sum of money and so they would send it that day. The figure was a few pounds more than the amount he'd just given away in church. Xander was understandably thrilled and thanked God for his generous provision *through* him and *to* him.

While writing this book a friend called Melanie has been going through a difficult divorce. Although her finances are restricted and uncertain, she told me that recently she felt she should give money to three different people, totalling £150, but was concerned that she might not have enough to live on for the month. She kept praying and thought it was the right thing to do although she didn't feel she had very much faith, but in the end she just gave and trusted that the Lord would look after her. The day after she'd given the final gift she received an unexpected letter from someone which included some money. The amount? £150! 'I was amazed. And so thankful,' Melanie told me. 'And the timing was wonderful. If it had come the week before, it would still have been good, but the fact that it came in *after* I'd given has strengthened my faith that the Lord is with me and looking after me, and will continue to do so.'

Give

The only way to see if God really does reward our giving, as Jesus says, is to do what Xander and Melanie and the Ephesian church did: give generously and see. This requires trust. Radical trust. Jesus knows there's a step of faith here, which is why he tells us to learn from the generous giving of the poor. This book has shown us, I hope, that this is more than just a step of blind faith into the total unknown, but a considered faith-step, based on the teaching of the Scriptures and the testimony and experience of the saints. Nevertheless, it still requires a deep trust that God will be true to his promises. Jesus – our Master in all things – modelled this generosity in his very life, with Paul describing him to the Corinthians in this way:

> Though he was rich, yet for your sake he became poor, so that you through his poverty might become rich.[53]

Jesus made himself poor, yet lived a life of generosity. He gave up the splendour of heaven and came to earth to give. He had no permanent home or regular income, yet he daily poured out his all for others. And on the cross, he offered up his life, giving us the greatest gifts of all: forgiveness and eternal life. In short, in his poverty Christ generously gave his all.

The widow of Jerusalem, who's been referenced in every chapter of this book, did something similar with her money. In her poverty she gave her all. In doing so she had to trust that God would look after her. Did he? We're not told. Her future is left wide open, which makes her story both fascinating and helpful because it allows us to identify while remaining curious. In the same way that we don't know how her future turned out, neither do we know for certain how it will be for us if we commit to giving like her. All we know is that God calls us to live generously, learning from the giving of the poor.

Look

Jesus knew that many would find this difficult, so having told his disciples in the Sermon on the Mount to give,[54] and not to 'store up . . . treasures on earth'[55] he then calls them to find inspiration for living this giving-trusting life from the natural world, which is where the Introduction to this book began. Here's what Jesus says:

> Look at the birds of the air; they do not sow or reap or store in barns, and yet your heavenly Father feeds them. Are you not much more valuable than they?[56]

If this is not enough, to be sure he gives a second illustration from creation:

> See how the flowers of the field grow. They do not labour or spin. Yet I tell you that not even Solomon in all his splendour was dressed like one of these.[57]

Jesus appeals to us to look beyond the apparent scarcity of our circumstances and observe the lavish bounty of creation, trusting that God will provide, for his bountiful generosity has been wonderfully built into the very fabric of his natural world.

So with Jesus, I invite you to observe the wonderous and overflowing created world in which we live, and then cultivate *The Art of Giving*. Give cheerfully, regularly, occasionally, collectively and expectantly. And if you haven't started yet, start today. For the God who made you is trustworthy, and has made a world that thrives on giving.

- while we give for the benefit of others, giving is good for us

- giving makes us happier, healthier, more neighbourly, more thankful, and can be infectious

- God will look after us as we give, including our financial needs

- we're called to be generous – not so we gain, but so we can give again and again

- generous giving involves radical trust that God will provide

Afterword

This has been the most difficult book that I've written to date. I've spoken on giving many times and so I thought when I sat down to write that it would be a fairly straight-forward process, but it's been far from that. As I've prayer-fully researched and read, listened to people's stories, and wrestled again with the Scriptures, this book has taken a number of drafts to produce. I hope it's better, more honest and more helpful as a result.

The present cost of living crisis affects us all and is a real challenge for most people in our nation and many across the world. In the UK today lots of people have less disposable income than they had four years ago. As a result some givers have reduced their giving, resulting in wonderful organisations like Christians Against Poverty having to lay off staff due to reduced income. This deeply saddens me. While I understand that cutting giving may be necessary for some, I do believe the call on God's church in difficult days is not to lower giving but rather to raise it, if we can. Give more, not less. For some this will mean that they have less savings. For others it might mean not replacing a device in the home when it breaks, or forgoing a holiday or some other desirable treat. The Lord will honour such costly and generous giving, and you might be surprised what he gives back. But the only way to find out is to learn the art of giving.

So let us give.

Acknowledgements

This book is dedicated to my fourth son, Isaac Porter. Isaac, you have a particularly generous and kind heart. As you seek to live daily as a disciple of Jesus, may you keep practising and modelling *The Art of Giving* in your everyday life, and thereby change the world.

I am so grateful to those who read initial manuscripts of this book, sharing their wisdom and reflections and making it better. These include: Jonathan de Bernhardt Wood, Brogan Hume, Vicky Earll, Ruth Somerville and John Valentine. Thanks, guys! You are greatly appreciated.

Resources

On Habits

James Clear, *Atomic Habits* (New York: Penguin, 2018).

Andrew Roberts, *Holy Habits* (Malcolm Down Publishing, 2016).

On Giving

Church of England Giving Survey, 2020: Top 10 Findings
https://d3hgrlq6yacptf.cloudfront.net/5fbc2ba5a8086/content/
pages/documents/anglican-giving-survey-poster.pdf

Jonathan de Bernhardt Wood, *Generosity – Fika Reflections*
https://www.churchofengland.org/sites/default/files/2021-06/gener
osity-fika-reflections.pdf

Jonathan Edwards, 'The Duty of Charity to the Poor', January 1732,
https://www.biblebb.com/files/edwards/charity.htm

Adam Grant, *Give and Take* (New York: Penguin, 2013).

Jack Hayford, *The Key to Everything* (Lake Mary, FL: Charisma
House, 1993, 2015).

R.T. Kendall, *The Gift of Giving* (London: Hodder & Stoughton, 1982,
2004).

Christian Smith and Hilary Davidson, *The Paradox of Generosity*
(Oxford: Oxford University Press, 2014).

Stewardship, *Simply Generous* (London: Stewardship, 2016).

John Stott and Chris Wright, *The Grace of Giving* (Peabody, MA: Hendrickson, 2016).

Paul Vallely, *Philanthropy: From Aristotle to Zuckerberg* (London: Bloomsbury, 2020).

On Money

John R. Muether, 'Money and the Bible', https://www.christianity-today.com/history/issues/issue-14/money-and-bible.html

Jay W. Richards, *Money, Greed and God* (New York: HarperOne, 2009, 2019).

Julian Richer, *The Ethical Capitalist* (London: Random House, 2018).

Justin Welby, *Dethroning Mammon* (London: Bloomsbury, 2016).

On Culture

Dan Gardner, *Risk* (London: Virgin, 2008).

Sendhil Mullainathan and Eldar Shafir, *Scarcity* (London: Penguin, 2013).

John Sentamu, *On Rock, Or Sand?* (London: SPCK, 2015).

Justin Welby, *Reimagining Britain* (London: Bloomsbury, 2018, 2021).

On Poverty

Martin Charlesworth and Natalie Williams, *A Church for the Poor* (Eastbourne: David C. Cook, 2017).

David Sheppard, *Bias to the Poor* (London: Hodder & Stoughton, 1983).

Ronald J. Sider, *Rich Christians in an Age of Hunger* (London: Hodder & Stoughton, 1977).

Notes

Preface

[1] Matthew 11:28–30. *The Message,* copyright 1993, 1994, 1995, 1996, 2000, 2001, 2002. NavPress Publishing Group.

Introduction

[1] Throughout the main text of this book most names of those in the stories told have been changed to preserve anonymity.

[2] For more on this see, for example, https://news.mongabay.com/2011/04/what-does-nature-give-us-a-special-earth-day-article/ accessed 6th February 2023.

[3] George Orwell, writing as an atheist in 1946, believed this, saying, 'The great mass of human beings are not acutely selfish. After the age of about thirty they abandon the sense of being individuals at all – and live chiefly for others . . .' George Orwell, *Why I Write* (London: Penguin, 1946, 2004), pp.4–5.

[4] Sociologist Robert Wuthnow recognises this, noting that the Hebrew Bible teaches that people are created in God's image and as such deserve all the care and kindness that can be given them; that The Koran says those who give to charity guard themselves from evil; that Buddhist thinking, especially in the Mayahana tradition, champions compassion above all other human qualities; and Christianity highlights love for neighbour, acts of mercy, and caring for people in poverty. (See Robert Wuthnow, *Acts of Compassion: Caring for Ourselves and Helping Others* [Princeton: Princeton University Press, 1991], p.122ff).

[5] By using this example of giving in a marriage relationship, I am not seeking to denigrate or in any way undermine singleness. The Bible celebrates singleness as a worthy state to be honoured, and indeed single people are called to give sacrificially to others in their relationships, as Christ did, who himself was single.

[6] https://www.churchofengland.org/prayer-and-worship/worship-texts-and-resources/common-worship/marriage#mm095 accessed 6th February 2023. Previous generations would have said these words in the form of the 1662 *Book of Common Prayer*, declaring: 'With this ring I thee wed, with my body I thee worship, and with all my worldly goods I thee endow: In the Name of the Father, and of the Son, and of the Holy Ghost. Amen.' See https://www.churchofengland.org/prayer-and-worship/worship-texts-and-resources/book-common-prayer/form-solemnization-matrimony accessed 6th February 2023.

[7] See Ephesians 5:25.

[8] See John 3:16, which shows that God is a 'giving God' whose generous nature is seen supremely in the giving of his Son, Jesus Christ. However, God's generosity is also revealed in creation itself (see Introduction) with Genesis 1 describing him creating *ex nihilo* ('out of nothing'). This is important, in that it shows how God's generous actions can take 'nothing' and from it make something of great worth, which continues to produce and provide. This echoes a key theme of this book – that God blesses the giving of poor people, taking their nothing and producing something of great value.

[9] See Colossians 1:15ff.

[10] This is perhaps best summarised in Psalm 65, which includes phrases such as 'You crown the year with your bounty, and your carts overflow with abundance' (v.11).

[11] Genesis 1:28.

[12] Genesis 1:31. Thus artist and theologian Makoto Fujimura says, 'There is not an iota of scarcity in "In the beginning, God created the heavens and the earth." The God of the Bible is the God of abundance' (Makoto Fujimura, *Art and Faith* (New Haven: Yale University Press, 2020), p.78.

[13] For more on scarcity, and especially how it becomes a mindset that takes root in people in poverty and also many affluent people, see Sendhil Mullainathan and Eldar Shafir, *Scarcity: The True Cost of Not Having Enough* (London: Penguin, 2013).

[14] Indeed basic economic theory teaches that we live in a world of unlimited demand and limited supply.

[15] Brené Brown, *Dare to Lead: Brave Work. Tough Conversations. Whole Hearts* (New York: Random House, 2018), p.120.

[16] Brené Brown, *Daring Greatly* (London: Penguin, 2012), p.18.

[17] Lynne Twist, *The Soul of Money: Transforming your Relationship with Money and Life* (New York: W.W. Norton & Company, 2017), pp.43–45.

[18] This 'space between' is sometimes described as *liminal space* – an uncomfortable place of transition but also of transformation. For an interesting perspective on this, related to the Covid pandemic, the church and mission, see Mark Bradford, *The Space Between* (Abingdon: The Bible Reading Fellowship, 2021). See also https://www.inaliminalspace.org/our-team accessed 24th February 2023.

[19] Matthew Porter, *Overflow* (Milton Keynes: Authentic Media, 2020), p.50.

[20] Source unknown. Widely attributed to the early medieval Catholic friar and mystic, St Francis.

[21] Timothy Keller, *Hope in Times of Fear* (London: Hodder & Stoughton, 2021), p.24.

[22] This is simply and beautifully summarised by John Stott and Chris Wright in the opening words to their book *The Grace of Giving*,

when they say, 'When we become Christians, our giving has a new impetus. We are called to give generously', John Stott and Chris Wright, *The Grace of Giving* (Peabody, MA: Hendrickson, 2016), p.3.

[23] Indeed 'grace' and 'generosity' can be used almost interchangeably, for 'Grace is another word for generosity'. Stott and Wright, *The Grace of Giving*, p.5.

[24] Brown, *Dare to Lead*, p.43.

[25] Michael Frost, *Surprise the World* (Colorado Springs, CO: NavPress, 2016) p.17ff.

[26] Justin Welby, *Reimagining Britain* (London: Bloomsbury, 2018, 2021), p.19.

[27] I don't especially like the term 'the poor' as it is sometimes used to label and identify people by their financial state. However, I will sometimes use it in this book, for three main reasons. First, for economic reasons. It sharply contrasts with 'the rich' and so draws attention to economic disparity, which is a huge issue in the twenty-first century, where the gap between the richest and poorest seems to be ever widening. Second, for historic reasons. It is a term that has been used by many down the ages to helpfully describe those who have very little. This is still the situation for many today. Third, for biblical reasons. It is a term used by Jesus and found in the Christian Scriptures.

In using the phrase 'the poor' I am not seeking to patronise or be negative about people in poverty; in fact quite the opposite is the case. I am seeking to draw attention to the stark reality that some have very little material wealth or goods, and there is much good to learn from them, especially when it comes to giving.

[28] A full and historical account of philanthropy is found in Paul Vallely's excellent work *Philanthropy: From Aristotle to Zuckerberg* (London: Bloomsbury Continuum, 2020).

[29] Heidi Baker, who has worked for many years with some of the
poorest people on the planet in Mozambique, agrees, saying, 'To
learn about hunger, sit with the starving. To learn about thirst, sit
with those who have nothing to drink.' Heidi Baker, *Compelled by
Love* (Lake Mary: Charisma House, 2008), p.59. She believes there
is much for rich disciples to learn by observing people in poverty,
when she writes, 'What is it about the poor that literally brings the
Kingdom of God in a way that the well-fed don't? It has to do with
hunger. It has to do with need. They know they need God. They're
hungry and thirsty. The Lord wants to cause even the rich, even the
middle-class, to be poor in spirit and know that they are in need
of Him' (Rolland and Heidi Baker, *Always Enough* [Grand Rapids:
Baker, 2003], p.165).

[30] Following the Church Fathers, including Ambrose (AD 340–397),
who said, 'Great indeed is that woman who was worthy to be pre-
ferred before everyone else according to the divine judgement!
Might it not be she who has drawn the two Testaments out of her
faith for the help of all humankind? Therefore, no one has done
more than she and no one has been able to equal the greatness of
her gift, since she joined faith to mercy. And you, too, whoever you
are . . . do not hesitate to bring to the treasury, two coins, full of faith
and grace' (see https://www.stathanasius.org/site/assets/files/3446/
study_04_26_15.pdf p.40 accessed 3rd March 2023. The importance
of this story to Christians today is seen in it appearing in BBC's 'Bi-
tesize' learning portal, as a key story in Christian discipleship about
sacrificial giving. See https://www.bbc.co.uk/bitesize/guides/
zvpfd6f/revision/9 accessed 3rd March 2023.

[31] The story also appears in Mark's gospel. As in Luke, it's set in the
context of warnings against the pride and vanity of the wealthy
teachers of the law. In Matthew we're also told that before the
widow gave, 'many rich people threw in large amounts' and yet

Jesus still says, 'This poor widow has put more into the treasury than all the others.' See Mark 12:41–44.

[32] Paul Penley: https://www.reenactingtheway.com/blog/the-widows
-mite-good-or-bad-example-of-giving accessed 1st March 2023.
See also, for example, http://www.pas.rochester.edu/~tim/study/
Widow%27s%20Mite.pdf accessed 1st March 2023.

[33] Jesus is following in the footsteps of prophets like Jeremiah – see
Jeremiah 23.

[34] On one occasion in Mark 7:11 Jesus condemns the religious leaders
for accepting gifts in the Temple that should have been spent on
looking after family, but this is more about giving and receiving
responsibly, rather than telling people *not* to give.

[35] This is one reason why provision for widows is an important theme
in the Bible: see Exodus 22:22–23; the book of Ruth; James 1:27. Two
significant stories of miraculous financial provision for widows
are: the Widow at Zarephath (1 Kings 17:7–24) and the Widow of a
Prophet (2 Kings 4:1–7).

Chapter 1

[1] Teresa of Avila, sixteenth-century Spanish nun and mystic. Cited in
J.M. Cohen, *The Life of St Teresa* (Edinburgh: Penguin, 1957), p.192.

[2] Maya Angelou, *Wouldn't Take Nothing for My Journey Now* (London: Bantam, 2011), p.11. Angelou (1951–2014) was an American storyteller, poet and civil rights activist.

[3] 2 Corinthians 9:7.

[4] Matthew 26:39.

[5] F.F. Bruce, *The Epistle to the Hebrews* (Grand Rapids, MI: Eerdmans, 1990), p.339.

[6] Jesus said this when he declared, 'Where your treasure is, there
your heart will be also' (Luke 12:34).

[7] Matthew 25:35–36.

[8] 2 Corinthians 9:11.

[9] This aspect of giving is often misunderstood, and has been much abused by so-called *prosperity gospel* teaching, which partly explains why it's an aspect of giving rarely discussed but, as we'll see, the Bible is clear on this and it is backed up by good empirical research.

[10] The New Testament sometimes says giving is like sowing seeds that can produce a great harvest, both 'on earth' for the present (2 Corinthians 9:10) and 'in heaven' for the future (Luke 12:33).

[11] Email to me from Jonathan de Bernhardt Wood, Church of England National Advisor on Giving and Income Generation, 11th July 2023.

[12] See Acts 16.

[13] Philippians 1:7.

[14] Philippians 1:4.

[15] Philippians 4:1.

[16] Philippians 1:18; 2:17; 4:10.

[17] Philippians 2:18; 3:1; 4:4.

[18] Philippians 4:11–12.

[19] Philippians 4:18.

[20] Philippians 4:19.

[21] Philippians 4:18.

[22] Luke 21:4.

[23] Psalm 100:2.

[24] See, for example, Deuteronomy 16:17 and 1 Corinthians 16:2.

[25] Acts 2:44.

[26] Acts 4:32.

[27] 2 Corinthians 8:2.

[28] Philippians 1:29–30.

[29] Philippians 2:4.

[30] Matthew 6:24.

[31] John R. Muether's paper 'Money and the Bible' has been helpful in giving historical context to differing views on money. For more on this, see https://www.christianitytoday.com/history/issues/issue-14/money-and-bible.html accessed 10th February 2023.

[32] Here's a quick summary. In medieval times some, following Thomas Acquinas in the thirteenth century, viewed money as a product of the fallen world and so inherently evil; so the best response was to either become poor, or to give away as much as possible. Later, John Calvin and other sixteenth-century Reformers, followed by the seventeenth-century Puritans, saw money more positively; they considered it to be a dynamic tool for the creation of wealth and to help the poor. Today there are a range of views about money with many sitting in the middle, considering money to be morally neutral. Martin Luther King, Jr. believed this, saying, 'Money, like any other force like electricity, is amoral and can be used for either good or evil' (see Martin Luther King, Jr., *A Gift of Love* [London: Penguin, 1963, 1981, 2012], pp.69–70). Those who take the neutral view would do well to hear the wisdom of C.S. Lewis, that 'a thing may be morally neutral and yet the desire for that thing may be dangerous' (*The Weight of Glory* by CS Lewis © copyright 1949 CS Lewis Pte Ltd. Extract used with permission). Some progressive thinkers take a more negative view today, with a number of liberation theologians considering money to be a 'power' that needs breaking (see, for example, Walter Wink, *Unmasking the Powers* [Philadelphia, PA: Fortress Press, 1984], p.28), and some seeing money as intrinsically demonic, which is why it's a tool used so often for selfishness and abuse, and it requires 'corporate exorcism' by revolutionary action (Wink, *Unmasking the Powers*, p.64). Whether you believe money

is inherently evil or not, this book commends the radical action of cheerful giving as a means of breaking its power.

[33] Pete Greig, *Dirty Glory* (London: Hodder & Stoughton, 2016), p.319.

[34] See, for example, Matthew 6:2–4 and Luke 18:9–14.

Chapter 2

[1] Rosario Butterfield, *The Gospel Comes with a House Key* (Wheaton, IL: Crossway, 2018), p.210. Butterfield is an author, homemaker and former professor of English at Syracuse University.

[2] James Clear, *Atomic Habits* (New York: Penguin, 2018), p.37. Clear is a writer and speaker focused on habits, decision making, and continuous improvement.

[3] Source unknown. Widely attributed to Aristotle, although for a view that it might be a summary of Aristotle, created by Will Durant, see https://medium.com/the-mission/my-favourite-quote-of-all-time-is-a-misattribution-66356f22843d accessed 24th February 2023.

[4] Adam Grant, *Give and Take* (New York: Penguin, 2013), p.179.

[5] Source unknown. Widely attributed to Franklin.

[6] 1 Corinthians 16:2.

[7] This is the consistent picture across the whole of Scripture. See, for example, Psalm 24:1–2; 1 Chronicles 29:14; Acts 17:24–28.

[8] Getting to grips with the biblical notion of *stewardship* can take some time, as I outline from experience in this chapter. The non-profit organisation *Generis*, which exists to encourage stewardship, helpfully describes five developmental stages in this giving journey, which many experience: 1) What do I do with my money? 2) What do I do with the money that God has given me? 3) What does God want me to do with what God has given me? 4) What does God want me to give from what God has given me? 5) What does God want me to keep from what God has given me? See generis.com accessed 23rd July 2023.

9 There are all sorts of songs that help us dedicate the whole of life and its resources to God, such as 'I Surrender All', 'Take My Life and Let It Be', 'I Will Offer Up My Life' and 'Be Thou My Vision'.

10 See Matthew 7:12; 10:42; Luke 16:19–31.

11 See Matthew 10:40–42; 25:34–46; Luke 14:12–14; 19:1–10.

12 See Matthew 9:10ff; Mark 2:15; John 12:2.

13 See Genesis 14:18–20. Christians should take this seriously, because Abraham is described in the New Testament as the father of faith (Romans 4:16; Galatians 3:9). Some argue that the tithe was part of the Old Testament 'law' that Christ abolished or fulfilled and so it is no longer a helpful principle. This is incorrect. The tithe was pre-law, and nowhere in the New Testament is it rescinded. This book argues that the tithe should not be followed legalistically but out of loving-obedience, and that it is a good starting point for giving; most, especially in the affluent West, can give more than a tithe, as we're invited to the higher calling of *generosity*.

14 By the time I was married my parents were comfortably off, and I knew if things were desperate I had a back-up plan and could ask them for help. This gave me an Option B. I recognise that many people from disadvantaged backgrounds have no Option B. While I am grateful for that option, since marriage I have felt it important to live independent of my parents. While they have occasionally given us financial gifts at their choosing, I have only once asked them for financial help. When my father died in 2005, my brothers and I inherited some money that allowed us to buy a property and gave us more financial stability. This allowed us to increase our giving, while seeking to live as simply as we can. Despite this, with a growing family of teenagers, we have since then still occasionally faced times of financial challenge, which have caused us to pray and trust the Lord. One such time has been when writing this book when, like many, costs have been high and disposable income squeezed.

15 For a few years when our children were small, my parents paid for some or much of a summer holiday for us, which we could not otherwise have funded.

16 Jonathan de Bernhardt Wood encourages this kind of approach, saying, 'I recommend trying every year to give 1% more of your net income away.' See https://www.churchofengland.org/sites/default/files/2021-06/generosity-fika-reflections.pdf p.5 accessed 24th July 2023.

17 'Your habits are not the only actions that influence your identity, but by virtue of their frequency they are usually the most important ones' (Clear, *Atomic Habits*, p.51).

18 Cited in R.T. Kendall, *The Gift of Giving* (London: Hodder & Stoughton, 1982, 2004), p.112.

19 Kendall, *The Gift of Giving*, p.112.

20 Kendall, *The Gift of Giving*, p.112.

21 See Malachi 3:6–12.

22 See John 12:6.

23 Money can do this. See, for example, Matthew 6:19ff.

24 See Mark 14:1–11. For a wider application of this text, on living a life of generosity, see https://www.churchofengland.org/sites/default/files/2021-06/generosity-fika-reflections.pdf accessed 24th July 2023.

25 See Matthew 27:1–10.

26 See my *The Art of Journalling* (Milton Keynes: Authentic Media, 2024).

27 'Less is more' is a phrase adopted in 1947 by architect Ludwig Mies van der Rohe. It can be applied in a variety of ways. Here I mean that by giving to less organisations we've been able to give more to each.

28 John Wimber, *The Way In is the Way On* (Eastbourne: Kingsway, 2007), p.70.

29   1 Samuel 16:7.

30   Malachi 3:8.

Chapter 3

1   Widely attributed to the eighteenth-century founder of the Meth-
     odist movement, John Wesley, and based on his sermon 'The Use
     of Money'. See https://s3.us-east-1.amazonaws.com/gbod-assets/
     generic/Use-Of-Money.pdf accessed 24th February 2023.

2   Speech given at the US National Prayer Breakfast, 3rd Febru-
     ary 1994. See https://www.ewtn.com/catholicism/library/mother
     -teresa-at-the-national-prayer-breakfast-2714 accessed 24th Feb-
     ruary 2023. Mother Teresa (1910–1997) founded the Missionaries of
     Charity, a Catholic organisation committed to caring for the poor-
     est people with dignity.

3   Craig S. Keener, *Acts: An Exegetical Commentary*, vol. 2 (Grand
     Rapids, MI: Baker Academic, 2013), p.1834.

4   Acts 11:29.

5   Acts 11:29.

6   See Acts 13:2–3.

7   David Watson, cited in ed. Jean Watson, *Each New Day with David
     Watson* (Crowborough: Monarch, 1988), p.338.

8   Matthew 6:10.

9   This three-fold process of discernment is sometimes described as
     revelation, interpretation and application. For more, see Matthew
     Porter, *A–Z of Discipleship* (Milton Keynes: Authentic Media, 2017),
     pp.48–49.

10   This is often a great challenge to those who have much, as the
     Scriptures consistently point out. See, for example, 1 Timothy 6:17;
     James 2:5; Matthew 16:24.

11   Acts 11:26.

12   See Acts 9:2; 19:9, 23; 22:4; 24:14, 22.

[13] There are other charities that do something similar, including Christian charity Stewardship.

[14] Matt Redman, 'Blessed Be Your Name' © Copyright 2002 Thankyou Music. See also my Discipleship Blog post entitled 'Pain in the Offering' https://matthewporter.blog/2014/01/21/pain-in-the-offering/.

[15] Matthew 6:2–3.

[16] John Grisham, novelist and former politician, cited in *Word in Action*, Winter 08, p.15.

[17] Matthew 25:31–46.

[18] Luke 14:13.

[19] Mark 10:21.

[20] For example: 'If anyone is poor among your fellow Israelites in any of the towns of the land that the LORD your God is giving you, do not be hard-hearted or tight-fisted towards them. Rather, be open-handed and freely lend them whatever they need' (Deuteronomy 15:7–8). 'Religion that God our Father accepts as pure and faultless is this: to look after orphans and widows in their distress and to keep oneself from being polluted by the world' (James 1:27). The Jerusalem elders said, 'We should continue to remember the poor, the very thing I had been eager to do all along' (Galatians 2:10).

[21] Edwards, 'The Duty of Charity to the Poor', Section I.

[22] https://cuf.org.uk/uploads/resources/Church-In-Action-Report.pdf accessed 23rd May 2023.

[23] Justin Welby, *Dethroning Mammon* (London: Bloomsbury, 2016), p.128.

[24] Welby, *Dethroning Mammon*, p.153.

Chapter 4

[1] https://www.latimes.com/archives/la-xpm-2000-jan-17-mn-54832-story.html#:~:text. accessed 21st February 2023. Loretta Scott King (1927–2006) was an American author, activist and civil rights leader

who was married to Martin Luther King, Jr. from 1953 until his assassination in 1968.

2 Grant, *Give and Take*, p.228.

3 Adapted from Paul Y. Cho, *Prayer: Key to Revival* (Waco: Word, 1984), pp.96–97.

4 https://www.christianitytoday.com/news/2014/february/founder-of-worlds-largest-megachurch-convicted-cho-yoido.html accessed 24th February 2023.

5 If true, it reminds us to consider the corrupting nature of money and to take seriously the advice of Deuteronomy 8, which warns God's people to take care when we prosper and wealth increases, and beware of complacency and forgetting the Lord and what he has done in the past.

6 Picking up Simon Sinek's famous phrase: 'Start with the Why' – see https://www.ted.com/talks/simon_sinek_how_great_leaders _inspire_action accessed 18th February 2023.

7 Ed. William Porter, *For Noble Purpose: The Autobiography of Richard Porter, Surgeon and Evangelist* (Ilkeston: Morleys, 2nd ed. 2006), pp.12–14.

8 Rev. Albert Barnes, *Notes on the Second Epistle to the Corinthians and the Epistle to the Galatians, Explanatory and Practical* (London: Gall & Inglis, 1850), p.201.

9 This is my translation of the Greek.

10 2 Corinthians 8:3.

11 Mark Batterson understands this, and similarly commends it, suggesting, 'If you give beyond your ability, God will bless you beyond your ability' (Mark Batterson, *The Circle Maker* (Grand Rapids, MI: Zondervan, 2011), p.55.

12 2 Corinthians 8:5.

13 Hebrews 10:24.

14 Eugene H. Peterson, *As Kingfishers Catch Fire* (Colorado Springs: Waterbrook, 2017), p.195.

[15] George Hunter III, *The Celtic Way of Evangelism* (Nashville: Abingdon Press, 2000, 2010), p.6.

[16] This is true in UK churches: see https://www.thetimes.co.uk/article/poor-churchgoers-more-generous-than-the-rich-h7rth-km8swl accessed 22nd February 2023. It's also true across the UK in general: see https://www.theguardian.com/society/2001/dec/21/voluntarysector.fundraising accessed 22nd February 2023.

[17] David Watson, *Discipleship* (London: Hodder & Stoughton, 1981, 1983), pp.21–22.

[18] See https://learn.tearfund.org/en/resources/footsteps/footsteps -71-80/footsteps-80/microfinance-programme accessed 2nd March 2022.

[19] Francis Martin, 'Survey Suggest 28-fold return on Tearfund projects', *Church Times,* 31st March 2023. https://www.churchtimes.co.uk/articles/2023/31-march/news/world/survey-suggests-28-fold-return-on-tearfund-projects accessed 20th May 2023.

[20] 2 Corinthians 8:7.

Chapter 5

[1] Christian Smith and Hilary Davidson, *The Paradox of Generosity* (Oxford: Oxford University Press, 2014), p.224. Reproduced by permission of the Licensor through PLSclear. Smith is a sociology professor at the University of Notre Dame, Indiana, and Davidson at the time of writing was a doctoral candidate in the sociology department.

[2] Welby, *Dethroning Mammon*, p.108. Justin Welby is the Archbishop of Canterbury.

[3] https://www.georgemuller.org/devotional/looking-to-the-lord-chapter-13 accessed 17th November 2022.

[4] See Luke 6:38.

[5] Psalm 112:5.

6　　2 Corinthians 9:10–11.

7　　Welby, *Dethroning Mammon*, pp.108–9.

8　　These five benefits are taken from https://greatergood.berkeley.edu/article/item/5_ways_giving_is_good_for_you accessed 12th November 2022.

9　　https://news.harvard.edu/gazette/story/2008/04/money-spent-on-others-can-buy-happiness/ accessed 13th November 2022.

10　　A 2006 study by Rachel Piferi of Johns Hopkins University and Kathleen Lawler of the University of Tennessee suggests a direct physiological benefit. See Rachel L. Piferi and Kathleen A. Lawler, 'Social support and ambulatory blood pressure: an examination of both receiving and giving', *International Journal of Psychophysiology*, November 2006, 62(2): 328–36. https://pubmed.ncbi.nlm.nih.gov/16905215/ accessed 23rd February 2023.

11　　According to Sonja Lyubomirsky, 'Being kind and generous leads you to perceive others more positively and more charitably' and this 'fosters a heightened sense of interdependence and cooperation in your social community' (Sonja Lyubomirsky, *The How of Happiness: A Practical Guide to Getting The Life You Want* [London: Piatkus, 2007, 2010], pp.129–30).

12　　See, for example, Smith and Davidson, *The Paradox of Generosity*, pp.74–78.

13　　Grant, *Give and Take*, p.56.

14　　Grant, *Give and Take*, p.182.

15　　Christian Smith and Hilary Davidson, *The Paradox of Generosity* (Oxford: Oxford University Press, 2014), p.224. Reproduced by permission of the Licensor through PLSclear.

16　　Malachi 3:10.

17　　Matthew 6:2, 4.

18　　This would concur with Malachi 3:11, which says that if we don't withhold our tithes and offerings, there will be some kind of preventative and protective benefit.

[19] Isaiah says something very similar in Isaiah 55:10 when he speaks of God sending down provision in the form of rain and snow to water the earth 'so that it yields seed for the sower and bread for the eater'. Seed is for us, so we are sustained, but also to plant and give away for the benefit of others.

[20] Stott is very helpful on this, saying, 'What we reap has a double purpose. It is both for eating and for further sowing . . . These verses are the origin of the concept of "seed-money," expecting God to multiply the donor's gift. Paul is not teaching a "prosperity gospel," as some have claimed. True, he promises that "you will be made rich in every way," but he adds at once that this is "so you can be generous on every occasion" (v11a) and so increase your giving. Wealth is with a view to generosity' (Stott and Wright, *The Grace of Giving*, p.27).

[21] https://st-bart.org/documents/2015/5/Caritas%20in%20Veritate.pdf Section 5, accessed 13th November 2022.

[22] See, for example, Chase Wagner, 'What Happens When We Worship?' *Influence Magazine*, 17th *November* 2016. https://influencemagazine .com/practice/what-happens-when-we-worship accessed 19th February 2023.

[23] See James 4:8.

[24] See, for example, https://www.theologyofwork.org/new-testament/ 2-corinthians/you-cant-outgive-god-2-corinthians-9 accessed 3rd March 2023.

[25] Batterson, *The Circle Maker*, p.52.

[26] Craig S. Keener, *Acts: An Exegetical Commentary*, vol. 3 (Grand Rapids, MI: Baker Academic, 2014), p.2815.

[27] See F.F. Bruce, *The Book of the Acts* (Grand Rapids, MI: Eerdmans, 1988), p.387.

[28] Acts 20:35.

29 Some doubt Paul's authorship, although I think it was most likely to be Paul. See Darrell Bock, *Ephesians: An Introduction and Commentary* (London: IVP Academic, 2019), p.10ff. Michael Cooper thinks Paul might have written it earlier, perhaps even between starting the church and his farewell speech; see Michael T. Cooper in *Ephesiology* (Pasadena, CA: William Carey Publishing, 2020), p.15.

30 Ephesians 3:16.

31 Ephesians 3:17–19.

32 Ephesians 6:24.

33 Stott and Wright, *The Grace of Giving*, p.5.

34 For more on the impact of the church in Ephesus, see Cooper in *Ephesiology, op cit.*

35 Peterson, *As Kingfishers Catch Fire*, p.197.

36 Matthew Porter, *Overflow* (Milton Keynes: Authentic Media, 2020).

37 This theme of *overflow* has been central to the ministry of Bill Johnson and Bethel Church in Redding, California. Johnson encourages people to be filled with the Holy Spirit, pointing out that 'fullness is measured in overflow' (Bill Johnson, *When Heaven Invades Earth* [Shippensburg: Destiny Image, 2003], p.75).

38 Jesus suggests in places such as Matthew 6:2ff and Luke 12:33 that there is a world of discovery that opens up when we give money, that doesn't come from other ways of giving.

39 Grant, *Give and Take,* p.183ff.

40 Grant, *Give and Take,* p.108.

41 Grant's *Give and Take* is one of the most helpful books on this. Interestingly, Grant urges givers not to become doormats, for many givers can be pushovers and be exploited, which can stop them reaching their full giving potential. This is especially true when applying generosity principles to the world of business, which is of great interest to Grant. Instead he argues that successful givers should beware of rigidly 'sticking with a single reciprocity style

across all interactions and relationships' and instead be flexible and focused in their giving (p.215).

[42] Luke 16:10–11.

[43] See, for example, Deuteronomy 15:10; Psalm 12:5; Galatians 2:10; James 1:27; 5:4.

[44] See, for example, Proverbs 21:13; 1 John 3:17–18.

[45] There are many psalms like this, which are often called 'Psalms of Lament', such as Psalm 63. For more on this, see Matthew Porter, *A–Z of Prayer* (Milton Keynes: Authentic, 2019) chapter S, where 'S is for Sad' (pp.141–6).

[46] See 2 Kings 4:1–7.

[47] See https://www.tearfund.org/about-us/what-we-do/church-and-community accessed 16th November 2022.

[48] Adapted from Graham Twelftree, *Drive the Point Home* (Crowborough: Monarch, 1994), pp.167–8.

[49] See John 15:13.

[50] Romans 12:15.

[51] Some of the issues in this section are similar to questions asked about unanswered prayer. For more on that, see 'U is for Unanswered' in my *A–Z of Prayer*, p.157–63.

[52] Jonathan Edwards, 'The Duty of Charity to the Poor', January 1732. https://www.biblebb.com/files/edwards/charity.htm accessed 24th October 2022.

[53] 2 Corinthians 8:9.

[54] Matthew 6:2.

[55] Matthew 6:19.

[56] Matthew 6:26.

[57] Matthew 6:28–29.

Authentic

We trust you enjoyed reading this book
from Authentic. If you want to be
informed of any new titles from this author
and other releases you can sign up to the
Authentic newsletter by scanning below:

Online:
authenticmedia.co.uk

Follow us: